No Self, No Problem
© 2006 Anam Thubten. All rights reserved.
Published by Dharmata Press, Point Richmond, CA 94807
Cover and book design by Ayelet Maida, A/M Studios
Author photograph by Jeffrey Roe
Printed in the United States of America
ISBN-10: 0-9788608-0-2 / ISBN-13: 978-0-9788608-0-6
06 07 08 09 10 / 5 4 3 2 1

no
self
no
problem

ANAM THUBTEN

Edited by Sharon Roe

DHARMATA PRESS
Point Richmond, California

The sky is always in a state of meditation.
The ocean is always in a state of meditation.
The universe is always in a state of meditation.
This is realized when self ceases.

—ANAM THUBTEN

❋

The sky is always in a state of meditation.
The ocean is always in a state of meditation.
The universe is always in a state of meditation.
This is realized when self ceases.

—Anam Thubten

✳

Dedicated to His Holiness Khenpo Jigmay Phuntsok
and my heart teacher Lama Tsur Lo

May luminous wisdom and compassion like theirs
shine brightly in the hearts of all beings.

Contents

Editor's Preface

I met Anam Thubten in 2002 shortly after he returned to the San Francisco Bay Area. At that time students were invited into his small living room on Saturday mornings for a short devotional practice followed by a talk.

The talks were always spectacular, startling and devoted to the most essential truths based on Rinpoche's personal experience of walking the spiritual path. They cut through layers of speculation, dissecting and challenging every fixed thought, every belief held as sacred truth. Rinpoche's target is always the heart of the matter which he clarifies in simple words accessible to Western thinkers without any knowledge of or commitment to Buddhism.

As the group of students grew, Rinpoche's living room became very crowded and sometimes students even sat out on the porch. Through the generosity of many benefactors we were able to purchase a historic chapel in the charming town of Point Richmond, California. I began transcribing Rinpoche's teachings and suggested that he publish a collection of Dharma talks. *No Self, No Problem* was born.

This book, based on talks given in 2005 and 2006 in Berkeley and Point Richmond, California, reflect Rinpoche's profound knowledge and insight into the human condition with clarity, humor and ruthless honesty. He shares his spiritual journey openly and honestly.

It has been an honor and a delight to work with and to present now to a wider audience the teachings of this authentic, simple and devoted man who has dedicated his life to expressing in words and actions profound messages of authentic wisdom and compassion.

—SHARON ROE

CHAPTER ONE

Pure Consciousness:
Our True Identity

We identify with our body made out of flesh, bones, and various components. Therefore we believe that we are material, substantial, and concrete. This has become an embedded belief system, so much so that we rarely question it. There are the inevitable conditions of old age, sickness, and death simply out of believing that we are this body. We always pay a high price whenever we believe in false perceptions. This perception is not just held individually. It is held dearly by the collective society and has been for many generations. That is why it is so strongly entrenched in our psyche. Our normal, every day perception of each other is governed by a false identity and then strengthened and enforced by the language we use.

At a very early age we are indoctrinated into this notion of self as the body. For example when we see a small child we say, "He is beautiful. I love his hair. She has the cutest eyes." Through thoughts and comments such as these we are planting the seeds of this mistaken identity. Of course there is nothing wrong with giving complements. It is much better than criticism. However it is still a form of misconception. The truth is that independent of any characteristics a child is inherently beautiful the moment she is born. So we are all beautiful.

We are living in an age where people are disconnected from their true identity and this false perception is validated from every angle. Everyone is craving a perfect body and seeking it in others. For example when you go to the grocery store you see that the magazines display pictures of men and women in a perfect and idealized youthful form. It is very difficult to resist these messages. They come from everywhere, all aspects of society and they validate this sense of mistaken identity. They validate the sense that this body is really who we are. Given the tendency to establish a perfect idealized standard many people suffer from pride, narcissism, arrogance, shame, guilt, and self-hatred because of their relationship with their body and their ability or inability to reflect this perfect standard.

Every morning when you wake up and look into the mirror, there is a voice in your mind. "Oh, another wrinkle." We are constantly judging ourselves and others according to this standard. Have you ever noticed that? Our mind is always judging people. "She is too fat. He is strange looking. She is beautiful. He is handsome." These judgments are not only creating a stumbling block on our spiritual path they are also creating clouds of negativity in our consciousness and keeping us firmly chained to the prison of duality.

But there is no need to hold onto this. There is the possibility of transcending this identification with our body in each and every moment. It is only when we drop all of these judgments that we will recognize that everyone is divine in their uniqueness. Egoic mind is always comparing self with others because it believes itself to be a separate entity and it uses body as the dividing line between self and other.

We are non-material. We are insubstantial. We are not like a table that breaks down eventually. The very essence of who we are goes beyond the conditions of decay and impermanence. Our body is impermanent but our true nature is not impermanent. Our true nature is deathless and divine, transcending all imperfections. Because of this we are all one and equal. Nobody is better or worse than anybody else. When someone manifests their true nature they live out of love, kindness, and joy. They inflict less pain on others. When you meditate then sooner or later you are going to discover that this is not just abstract theory. This corresponds to the truth, to reality.

What is our true nature if it is not this body? There are many words we can use to describe what our true nature is. The simplest word is Buddha nature. The definition of Buddha nature is that we are already enlightened. We are perfect as we are. When we realize this, we are perfect. When we do not realize this, we are still also perfect. Our true essence goes beyond birth and death. It can never get sick. It can never get old. It is beyond all conditions. It is like the sky. This is not a theory. This is the truth that can only be realized in the realm of enlightened consciousness. This consciousness is surprisingly accessible to each of us.

When that awakening happens there is no longer any desire to become someone other than who we are. Every previous idea of who we are vanishes, along with it the pain, guilt, and pride associated with our body. In Buddhism this is called *no self*. This is the only true awakening. Everything else is a spiritual bypass. This awakening is what you should be aiming toward from the very beginning of being on the path. It will rescue you from falling into unnecessary spiritual traps. When we are open hearted and ready to drop our previous perceptions of self, then spiritual awakening can happen at any moment.

There is a beautiful analogy. Imagine a dark cave that hasn't been illuminated for a million years. Then one day someone brings a candle into the cave. Instantaneously the darkness of a million years vanishes. Like that, when your true nature is realized there is no longer this *I* searching for anything else. The awakening has nothing to do with your background. It has nothing to do with whether you have been meditating for a long time or not. It has nothing to do with meeting impressive teachers or gurus. It is simply dependent on whether or not you are open to it.

This opening, this receptivity is basically related to our ability to resist arming the ego with concepts and ideas. A true spiritual path transcends all concepts and belief systems. It is not about re-enforcing the mind's illusion of self as an identity. It is not about being "a Buddhist, a saint, or a better person." It is really about deconstructing all of our illusions without any mercy.

It is very important to look into your mind to see what you are looking for, what you are seeking. This is especially relevant when you are going to receive spiritual teachings. When a spiritual teacher impresses you, you might discover that your desire is completely antagonistic to authentic awakening. Perhaps your mind is looking for comfort, for validation, for a spiritual high, or new set of belief systems. Sometimes your ego convinces you that you are realizing this sense of no fixed self but simultaneously you are holding on to another concept like being sacred or being spiritual. Holding on to concepts such as sacred or spiritual while we are working towards transcending self-attachment is very subtle.

Perhaps this sounds like a lot of work, like an arduous insurmountable task. It isn't when you find the secret ingredient. That is to know that this *I* is a fictitious entity that is always ready to whither away the moment you stop sustaining it. You don't have to go to any holy place to experience this. All you have to so is simply sit and pay attention to your breath, allowing yourself to let go of all fantasies and mental images. Then you can experience connecting to your inner world.

As you begin to rest and pay attention you begin to see everything clearly. You see that the self has no basis or solidity. It is a complete mental fabrication. You also realize that everything you believe to be true about your life is nothing but stories fabricated around false identifications. "I am an American. I am thirty years old. I am a teacher, a taxi driver, a lawyer...whatever." All of these ideas or identities are stories that never really happened in the realm of your true nature. And watching the dissolution of these individual stories is not painful. It is not painful to see everything dissolving in front of you. It is not like watching your house burn down. That is very painful because you don't want to loose everything. Spiritual dissolution is not like that because what is being destroyed is nothing but this sense of false identities. They were never real in the first place.

Try this. Pay attention to your breath in silence. Look at your mind. Immediately you see that thoughts are popping up. Don't react to them. Just keep watching your mind. Notice that there is a gap between each thought. Notice that there is a space between the place where the last thought came to an end and the next one hasn't arrived yet. In this space there is no *I* or *me*. That's it.

It might be hard to believe how simple it is to realize the truth. As matter of fact, a Tibetan lama named Mipham Rinpoche said that the only reason we don't realize the truth is because it is too simple. If we look around carefully, there are hundreds even thousands of indications proving this notion that self is unreal. Look at face of newborn child, a flower blossoming beautifully in a garden, they're all pointing toward this mystical realization.

You might like to apply this simple inquiry whenever problems arise. If you feel angry or disappointed, simply ask who is the one being angry or disappointed. In such inquiry, effortlessly inner serenity can manifest.

There are stories about people who have been struggling with life's problems for a very long time without resolution. Once they sat down and asked themselves who is struggling they realized that there was never a problem from the beginning. In a true sense this is the only solution that helps us. Everything else is just a patch that gives us a false sense of liberation for a short while. How many times have we tried these temporary fixes and solutions? Are we exhausted yet? If everybody on the planet, including politicians, businessmen and religious leaders started working toward this realization then the world would immediately be a peaceful place. People would be much kinder and more generous toward each other.

When all the layers of false identity have been stripped off there is no longer any version of that old self. What is left behind is the pure consciousness. That is your original being. That is your true identity. Your true nature is indestructible. No matter, whether you are sick or healthy, poor or wealthy, it always remains divine and perfect as it is. When you realize your true nature, your life will be transformed in a way you could not have imagined before. You'll realize the very meaning of your life and it will also put an end to all searching right there.

Many people are looking for the perfect life in the distant future while they're busy wasting each moment of their precious life fabricating mental and psychological problems. We should remember that each moment is a thresh-hold to perfect awakening. Awakening to our true nature is the key to unlocking the door of the paradise that lies within each of us. Paradise is not some kind enchanted land filled with flowers and music. It is not some kind of spiritual Disneyland. Paradise is our primordial pure consciousness that is free of all limitations, but embodies the infinity of the divine. I remember seeing a bumper sticker that said, "I believe in life before death." To me this means that we don't have to imagine a future paradise. Paradise can happen right here, right now, while we're in this human incarnation. This depends on our own choice.

CHAPTER TWO

Meditation:
The Art of Resting

It is very good to ask from time to time "What am I searching for?" This is a very powerful question. It may surprise and shock you when you figure out what you have been up to. It turns out that often we figure out that we have been chasing after illusions. Sometimes they are beautiful illusions like the illusion of enlightenment and spiritual transformation but as long as we allow our mind to chase after such illusions there is no true liberation. There will be spiritual highs but no true liberation.

It is very easy to have spiritual highs. Sometimes they are very pleasant, like drinking wine. When we get depressed sometimes we like to drink wine or sometimes we get out of bed at one or two o'clock in the morning and stuff ourselves with ice cream. Having spiritual highs is a bit like that. It's just an anti-depression, anti-conflict, anti-sadness technique because it doesn't really cut the root of suffering in the ultimate sense. So we have to make sure that what we are searching for is not just another beautiful illusion. There are a lot of illusions. Life is run by illusions, believe it or not. One time Buddha Shakyamuni said, "I have never been born and I have never taught even one word." This was the most profound teaching that he has ever given. What he meant is that everything is an illusion. That is the truth whether our mind can digest that as truth or not. Even Buddha himself is an illusion.

In the same way when you look into your own consciousness you see that your mind is always telling you all kinds of stories. Everything that you believe to be reality is nothing more than stories. "I was born in 1953 or 1963. I went to such and such college. I married. I divorced. I had children. I did this and that. I met with a great teacher two years ago and I found the path to liberation." It's all a story, all an illusion. The truth is nothing is happening. Therefore we have to make sure that this egoistic mind is not just chasing after illusion again.

Have you ever noticed that you have a tremendous sense of fear and resistance when you believe that you are losing something? We always lose in our life. We lose our loved ones. We lose our job. Sometimes we lose love from other people and sometimes we lose our fantasies. We are constantly losing. Eventually we lose this body too. We lose this entire universe when we lose this body. This is called death. Whether we can accept it or not the truth is that sooner or later we are going to lose everything when we die without any choice. No matter how beautiful our illusions are they are all illusions.

The beautiful illusion that is unfolding right now will soon be lost. There is not even one single illusion that we can hold on to forever. We are going to lose everything sooner or later. The sense that it will last is only our mind telling us stories. Illusion is unreal. Illusion is mental projection. It does not have any concrete or inherent reality. When we look we see that egoistic mind is perpetuating this tendency to search for illusions, all kinds of illusions. And it has done this for many lifetimes.

True realization is knowing that everything is an illusion. Without having that realization there is no freedom. Therefore the goal of the path of Buddha Dharma is to bring about that realization in our mind and to live each and every moment in that realization. The goal is not just having that realization periodically but living that realization as a way of life. Sleeping in that realization. Eating in that realization. Taking a shower in that realization. Fighting in that realization sometimes. That's okay too as long as everything is happening in the context of that realization. It's not that you always have this beautiful smile and are dancing all of the time when you live in such true realization. You still have to engage in earthly reality.

Realization is the heart of awakening. Without that there is no freedom. There is no liberation. Even though we think that we are transforming and that we are getting somewhere actually we are just having another spiritual high, another spiritual illusion. The truth is that no transformation happens as long as there is no realization. So the real question is how can we realize the truth? How can we realize that everything is nothing but illusion especially when we feel that our suffering is very real? How can we realize that all of the negativities such as illness and unwanted conditions are simply illusion? It is also not easy to realize that everything is illusion when we are having a good time. Sometimes after we meditate we have a glimpse of this truth that everything is an illusion. But when we get off our cushion and begin to deal with everyday life it is very easy to lose that realization.

Sometimes this egoistic mind has a tendency to work very hard trying to get somewhere, trying to realize the truth right now. It sounds very good especially since I have been saying that this realization is the source of freedom. Ego will tell you, "This is good. I'm going to go after spiritual realization. I am going to do everything I can in order to get that as a spiritual reward." Ego will tell you to search for more knowledge, more esoteric knowledge, and more training, more spiritual complexity. And then ego will tell you that if you keep collecting more complicated spiritual information, more exact techniques, more techniques that are difficult to perform, the more profound it is. Ego tells you that the harder it is, the better it is. The more nonsense, the more mumbo-jumbo there is, the more sacred it is. And therefore this ego sometimes becomes a workaholic trying to figure out various spiritual training methods and gathering all of this conceptual information. Then it thinks, "Oh I am getting somewhere now because I am paying the dues. I am working hard." But the truth is that it never works that way. Sometimes these spiritual complexities and spiritual disciplines can be a hindrance blinding your consciousness from what is already there.

So you might like to ask the question, "What is really the perfect path to awakening?" Of course there is no 'only way' or 'perfect way' to the path of awakening. I always like to remember the image of Buddha Shakyamuni sitting for six years. This led him to awakening. Therefore sometimes the best thing that we can do is to just rest and relax. Ego may tell us, "That's too simple. Spirituality cannot be simply relaxing. There must be something more than that." But actually ultimately it's all about relaxing. Therefore many Buddhist masters define meditation as the art of resting or the art of relaxing.

When we relax completely we see that all of our thoughts start to dissipate. The egoistic mind begins to dissolve automatically. The egoistic mind is very powerful and if we try to get rid of it, it doesn't really work. But when we just sit and relax it dissolves without doing anything. Somehow we have the idea that ego is the troublemaker. Especially if you are Buddhist you may believe that ego is the troublemaker. We have names for the ego like Mara, which means the cosmic devil. That is the worst name you can give to anybody and that is the name given to the ego. Because we have been criticizing and bashing the ego all of these years we think that we have to fight against it, resist it and transcend it. The truth is the more we try to transcend ego the stronger it becomes. It's just like when you tell somebody *not* to think about a monkey. They end up having to think about a monkey. Therefore sometimes it's good to just let go of all of the effort of trying to conquer and get rid of ego and just rest. It is so simple. Everybody knows how to rest.

This kind of message is not really a new message. It's a very old message, an age-old message. The message is that if we just rest in this natural state of consciousness, in this very present moment, then this awareness, this realization that everything is an illusion sometimes just pops up automatically. It is very easy for people to think well, this is my first time meditating. This is the first time that I am hearing Buddhist teachings so how can I expect realization on the spot. Or some people may think that they don't know how to meditate or haven't received enough teachings so they cannot experience awakening on the spot. There are all kinds of excuses not to awake right now. Actually we all know how to awake because we all know how to rest.

Meditation is about resting completely. Not just physical rest but complete rest. Rest that includes letting go of all forms of mental effort. Mind is always busy doing something. Mind has a very huge job to do. It has to sustain the universe. It has to sustain existence because if your mind collapses then there is no universe. Just like the Heart Sutra says there is nothing there. There is no Nirvana. There is no Samsara. There is no suffering. There is no imprisonment. There is nothing there when mind stops maintaining this virtual reality. There is no universe. It's like riding a bicycle. When you ride a bicycle you have to keep pedaling constantly. If you pause and stop pedaling the bicycle doesn't run on its own. It just falls down. In the same way as long as we don't create this imaginary world, this imaginary reality, then it collapses right there. Whatever you call it, Samsara, reality or illusion, it collapses. It collapses because there is no one there working constantly to perpetuate it. Therefore mind feels that it has a big responsibility. It feels that it has to constantly construct and perpetuate this world of illusion.

So to rest means to pause, to pause from working very hard, to pause from continuously constructing this world of illusion, the dualistic world, this world that is based on the separation between self and other, you and me, good and bad. When you completely take away the egoistic mind, the creator of this illusory world, then the realization is already there. Then truth is automatically realized. Therefore the heart of Dharma is to relax and to rest. We think that we know how to rest. When you meditate you discover that the mind has a tendency to always work to always exert effort, to always attempt to gain control of reality. Mind is not completely peaceful and relaxed. You find different layers of mind's effort. It is very amazing to notice when you sit that sometimes you think at first, "Oh, my mind is completely serene and peaceful." If you keep paying attention to your consciousness you see that there is a very subtle effort. This is the mind's effort of trying to have control over reality. Maybe mind is seeking enlightenment. Maybe mind is trying to transcend ego. Maybe mind is saying, "I don't like what I am experiencing right now. There is pain in my joints." Maybe mind is trying to . . . whatever . . . finish the meditation session. Mind is always making up stories. It's always writing this cosmic script. Therefore this notion of resting is to let go of all of this. Let go of all thought. Let go of all of mind's effort and completely be in that natural state of your mind, the truth, or the what is, and then there is already realization.

Sometimes it is very beautiful to just sit. Buddhist training begins by practicing sitting meditation just like Buddha Shakyamuni who sat for many, many years. This is the package deal that comes along with being on the Buddhist path. Sooner or later we all have to dedicate an amount of time to sitting. I always encourage everybody to take some time from everyday life to sit. You can sit for twenty minutes or forty minutes or one hour or for a few hours.

I used to give meditation cushions to students and at first people were really happy to receive them. Then I tell them that actually this is a package deal. It's like those advertisements we sometimes receive in the mail. You know the ones that say we are going to receive a free credit card or some kind of gift. At first we are so happy that we are about to dance. Then after we read a few sentences we see that it is a package deal. There are some strings attached to the deal. Just like that there is a package deal with the meditation cushions. The deal is that you must meditate every day for six months. People are already attached to that meditation cushion and it's too late for them to change their minds. So I am thinking about having this little Dharma gift. Perhaps the meditation cushions are too cumbersome for me to carry around in an airplane. Perhaps I will use something nice and simple like a Mala or a beautiful image. At first you will be so happy to receive it that you will be ready to dance, and then I will say wait a moment. It's not the end of the story. There is a package deal here. You have to meditate for another six months.

So the heart of Buddhist training is to practice meditation. What is meditation? It is simply the art of resting and relaxing. I always like to tell this story. The story is about a monkey who came to the place where Buddha was meditating in a perfect posture. Buddha was in deep silence without any movement so the monkey did not know whether he was alive or dead. Buddha was so relaxed that when the monkey tickled him he did not react. Finally the monkey began to imitate him. He sat in this perfect posture with crossed legged and his head bent down a little bit. He began to pay attention to his breath and soon he became enlightened on the spot. This is a very beautiful story. It is profound and it is also very simple. Basically the story is telling us that the very heart of Dharma is not complicated. It is not effortful. It is too simple and that's why it is difficult sometimes to appreciate sitting meditation.

When I went to the monastery I did lots of sitting meditation and I thought that this sitting meditation is not enough because there are no fireworks. Nothing special is happening. Also when somebody asks you what you have been doing it is very embarrassing to say, "Oh, I was just sitting." It is much more powerful to say that I have finished this list of things. It is very nice to present a list of your achievements but it can be very embarrassing to tell somebody I was just sitting. I was sitting for six months or I was sitting for one year. It is very embarrassing for ego to report this as so called spiritual achievement.

I believe that once you discover an affinity with sitting meditation it means that you are very close to awakening. So try to develop an affinity with sitting meditation. Just sit every day. First you are going to have all kinds of reactions to just sitting. Ego is going to try to convince you that just sitting is not good enough. Ego is going to create lots of busy-ness, lots of resistance. Either you are too busy or you don't have enough time or you have difficulty getting up in the early morning. Sometimes you experience procrastination. Your ego tells you, "Today I don't have time to meditate maybe tomorrow I will meditate. Or maybe in one month I will meditate." The ego is always creating all kinds of resistance, subtle as well as gross resistance to prevent you from developing this regular meditation practice. So in the beginning you have to force yourself to meditate. Sometimes you can make a vow to meditate every day.

If you are really serious about awakening, if you are really serious about discovering true realization, then you have only one choice and that is to practice meditation every day as the number one priority in your life. It is often good to make a commitment. Therefore it was very nice when I gave these meditation cushions to people. When they sat, the cushion reminded them that they had a commitment to sit for six months. Sometimes it is very good to vow either in the presence of a Dharma teacher or even in front of a sacred image such as Buddha Shakyamuni.

The heart of the Dharma teaching is to encourage everybody to meditate. Meditation is simply the art of resting and relaxing. That's how simple it is. It is so simple that we feel that it cannot be the ultimate message of the Dharma. The rest that I am speaking about is a deep rest, an inner rest, a rest in which you let go of all forms of mind's effort including mind's effort to maintain this illusory self.

When you look at that sacred image of Buddha make a vow that you are gong to mediate every day from now on and that you are going to carry this awareness and this enlightened mind each and every moment while you are meditating and while you are going about the business of everyday life. We can make a commitment and dedicate our life and our heart to complete and everlasting awakening. When you make that vow then you find that there is a strength in each of us that allows us to overcome all of the resistance, all of the strategies set by ego to jeopardize our path to awakening. That inner strength helps us to overcome fear, insecurity, doubt and distraction. It helps us overcome everything.

CHAPTER THREE

Inner Contentment:
Giving Up Nothing But Attachment

There are many distorted versions of happiness. Happiness is a goal that we all want even though we don't admit that sometimes. It is the very reason we are on the path. It is also the reason we are pursuing activities such as careers, relationships and all kinds of accomplishments. All of our activities are motivated by attempts to bring about the happiness we all desire, so it is good to admit that we all want happiness.

Sometimes we tend to get a little pretentious in terms of admitting that we want happiness. It sounds shallow or unsophisticated and since we are spiritual seekers we should at least have the pretense that we want awakening or enlightenment more than happiness. But at the bottom of everything that's what we all desire. There is nothing wrong with wanting happiness but we have to define what true happiness really is. That is a very important step.

Happiness is not something we can achieve by accumulating things, or by realizing our beautiful illusions. Rather contentment is inner. Contentment is not the state of having everything. It is the state where attachment and fear are completely absent. That is contentment. Contentment is a state of mind where ongoing obsessive desire "I want this; I want that;" has completely ceased. So actually this is a state of emptiness rather than a state of having everything that you have been fantasizing about and longing for.

Let me give an analogy. If you want to create space here in the room and you start bringing in a lot of stuff from the outside it would not work out. Your whole place would become stuffed with junk so how are you going to create space? You must begin to get rid of things. Get rid of all the junk. Get rid of all of the things that are not necessary. In the same way to bring about contentment we need a consciousness that is like creating space. It's not about having more, accumulating more. Rather it is about letting go of this and that, letting go of everything. And then space is already there. Inner contentment is already there and that is true happiness. There is no enlightenment other than that.

The true spiritual path involves bringing about contentment through letting go of all attachment. That's why the very essence of Buddha's teaching is called non-attachment. Buddha even defined Dharma as the path of non-attachment. But there is a big difference between giving up everything and giving up the attachment to everything. I don't think that we have to go in the direction of even trying to give up everything. That's impossible anyway. We can't give up everything. There are many things that we can't give up. It's obvious we can't give up our basic necessities. We need a home, food, clothes and so forth. When we look at it eventually we realize that actually we can't give up anything. And this is all right.

For example when I travel I always try to reduce the size of my suitcase. So I fumble through all of my belongings and try to bring very few things. I look through everything. My toothbrush? I really have to take that. Shaver? I need that. Eventually I realize that I can't leave anything behind. It always seems that the process of giving things up is like the process of packing my suitcase. So you don't have to give up anything at all. As a matter of fact this path is about returning everything, returning all of your pleasure and enjoyment as a source of non-attachment, which is very ironical. But if you have a mind of knowing how to transcend attachment inwardly then this makes sense. Otherwise this doesn't make sense.

There is a story about the great Indian King Indrabodhi. One day he went to Buddha and asked, "I want to find liberation. What should I do?" Buddha said, "From this moment on you must take ordination. You must become a monk." Then Indrabodhi said that he would rather be born as a fox living in a beautiful valley than become a monk. He said, "Please show me a path to liberation where I don't have to give up anything. I don't have to give up my palace, my power, my relationships." And the teaching says that Buddha taught him a path and let him become enlightened without having to give up anything.

The heart of spiritual practice is letting go of everything inwardly. It requires a very special understanding because it can be tricky. You can have everything but you cannot get attached to anything. Who can do that? You can eat ice cream but you can't get attached to it. Strawberry ice cream, we eat it and we get attached to it. We want more. It's not healthy to get attached to strawberry ice cream because it could be the last time we have it. When we are attached we crave more. We feel that we must have more. We just can't function without having more of that strawberry ice cream. We remember how delicious it was and also sometimes we use it as a kind of anti-depression device. So this can be challenging. You can have everything. You don't have to give up anything. And at the same time you can't get attached to anything. This can be very challenging.

We have to remember that non-attachment is the only path to the great liberation. There isn't any other way. But it is absolutely up to us how we are going to undertake that path. There is not just one path. There is no particular way, no perfect way to non-attachment. There are many ways, hundreds of ways that we can undertake the path of non-attachment. Sometimes people like monks and nuns give up everything. That is their way of renouncing attachment. And sometimes we simply don't give up anything. Just like King Indrabodhi we keep everything we have been protecting, our career, possessions, lifestyle, position, relationships, and projects. We keep it all without giving up even one single thing. And still if you understand the very heart of Dharma then you are practicing non-attachment by letting go of your obsession and your identification with everything inwardly rather than outwardly.

Let me get to the heart of the matter. What would be the most skillful and effective way for all of us to undertake the path of non-attachment especially if we try to find the path of the perspective of the middle way, not falling into any extremes of either indulgence or fanatical austerity? What would be the perfect way to the path of non-attachment in our everyday life? I believe that it is necessary to give up certain things in our life even physically and externally. This has nothing to do with practicing austerity. As a matter of fact I do not recommend that people take a path of renunciation like a monk or nun unless they have a very true desire, a real heartfelt longing to be a monk or nun. Otherwise that kind of lifestyle is not recommended for us. Especially for those who are living in a modern world it is very challenging to become a monk or nun.

At the same time it is very good to renounce one thing. Renounce something that serves as a distraction and indulgence keeping you from facing reality, some reality that you have been trying to avoid. There is a part of us that is very scared and in a way a coward. And this part of us puts up great resistance because we don't want to go though the final ultimate test, to let go of all illusion and become awakened. There is always a final test waiting for us that we have to go through to become fully awakened, fully enlightened. If you are able to face that ultimate challenge, then you will be awakened right now. And if you allow yourself to go through the whole process without running away, without changing your mind, and without hiding behind all of these psychological masks of resistance, then enlightenment can happen right now in a single instant. This is not a theory. This is not simply a speculation. This happens and it has happened to many great, extraordinary enlightened masters throughout history.

So anyway you have to observe truthfully, honestly. What sort of habits or indulgences or attachments are you using as a way of running away from the encounter with reality. It can be anything. It's quite surprising. You can be quite shocked to discover what you have been using to avoid reality. Sometimes even very simple behaviors and activities in our lives can be used as a shield against reality. Things like watching TV, reading newspapers or books, or gossiping on the phone. Watching TV in particular can be a great source of distraction. I am not saying that watching TV is sinful, not at all. I'm sure that there are wonderful educational programs on TV. But usually people tend to use TV as a way of distracting themselves from facing their own reality, their own shadow, their own inner sorrow and loneliness. They often use TV as a way of escaping from that sometimes very frightening reality.

Especially if you are somebody who has been watching TV for a long time you will find sometimes that it is very challenging to be without these distractions for even one or two days. You will find that it is quite challenging. There is almost a desperation in your life right there. You may find that you almost cannot face the loneliness. It is very painful to be with that because you are no longer distracting your mind from facing reality. Whatever there is. So my recommendation as a method of bringing about the wisdom of non-attachment is to really go through your lifestyle, your habits. Go through all of your usual activities and you will find that there are a lot of tendencies that we use to shield ourselves from facing reality. And once you are able to pinpoint what that is then you have to be very serious, deadly serious, and you have to practice refraining from that specific habit whether it is watching TV too much, reading too much, chatting too much, drinking alcohol too much, or smoking cigarettes. Whatever it is.

Just pick one thing that you are really holding on to, one personal habit that you really cling to as a kind of refuge and try not to indulge in that habit. This is good to do even if you cannot give it up completely. There are certain things that we cannot give up completely because life would not operate. For example making phone calls is so necessary in this twenty first century that it is almost impossible to operate our lives without relying on the telephone. And that's why there is no need to completely give up the telephone. But at the same time if you realize that one of your tendencies to distract your mind is to be on the phone constantly and to chat and to gossip then it will be quite transformational and liberating to just reduce that habit and try not to use the phone as you have been doing in the past. And that can be a discipline, a perfect Dharma practice. So Dharma practice is not always sitting on a meditation pillow.

For example one could say, "My teacher told me that I should sit for twenty minutes every day and meditate. Since I am doing that then after that I can do whatever I want to do. It is beyond the realm of Dharma." When this is the case then the realm of Dharma is very tiny and the realm of Samsara is the size of the whole world. So we deliberately on our own, without any provocation, end up extending the realm of Samsara so we can indulge our habits. We can be very ordinary. We can throw our emotions around at other people. We can be mean, nasty and passive–aggressive toward other people. We can be very ordinary and mediocre. As spiritual seekers we have to integrate spiritual practice with everyday life where awareness and mindfulness bless our activities and interactions with ourselves and other people in each and every moment. Then our delusions and suffering begin to wither away.

Actually in the beginning you may have to struggle a little especially if you are really getting onto the path of non-attachment for the first time in a serious way. There will be a little struggle. It won't be a terrible struggle at all. But there will be moments when you will notice that you have failed one time after another. Sometimes you feel that you have failed so much in the practice of non-attachment that you think that this is just not working out for you so you are going to give it up completely. Actually failing is absolutely fine because we have already completely and utterly failed. Why are we afraid of failing again? We have failed so completely that we have lost the sense of who we are. We have lost the realization of who we are. We have lost our unity with our true nature. That is the greatest failure. Nothing else is really a tragedy or a real serious failure in comparison with the failure of losing our unity with our true nature. This has already happened to all of us from the very beginning and that is why it is impossible to really fail again. Any subsequent failure is just an idea. "Oh I am losing my job. I failed. I didn't pass my test. I failed again. My relationship is falling apart. I failed again. My meditation is filled with turbulence. I failed. I wasn't able to live the life that I fantasized. I am not able to live in accordance with my ideal standards. I failed." These are all concepts.

The true failure is that we have lost our unity with our true nature. Beyond that there is no failure. Everything else is simply a perception an idea. Of course we can live in that illusion of failure forever and then torment ourselves day after day. Sometimes our mind is the greatest challenge we face, more challenging than anything we face from the outside. Our mind can be very destructive, very dangerous. Our mind can be our greatest adversity especially when our mind chooses to live in unenlightened perceptions of reality. You can eat a lot of food, you can live a beautiful life but still you will not be content as long as you are living in unenlightened perceptions. So failure is just a perception, that's all. It is okay to fail and to fail continuously time after time. In fact every time you fail you should give yourself a chocolate as a reward. Then you will start to think failure is okay because you will get a reward. We can reverse the idea of failure and reward. We can do that. Why not? So it's okay to fail because we have already failed from the beginning.

There is going to be a stage in your meditation practice when your strong attachment to hope and fear are going to completely disappear from your consciousness and you will find a sense of certainty in yourself and also in the very journey that you are on. From that moment on even when you encounter emergencies, moments of fear, terror, loneliness, desperation you will not completely lose your sense of inner serenity. Eventually through cultivation of meditation, non-attachment and mindfulness, your serenity is always going to be there as majestic as a mountain. A mountain is so majestic that it can maintain in the face of an earthquake, in the face of a storm, in the face of thunder and lightening. In the same way you are going to be able to stabilize awareness that is like a mountain regardless of all that is happening outside of your consciousness and within your consciousness. Your awareness will be stabilized and eventually you will no longer identify yourself with conditions.

Right now we are identifying ourselves with conditions. That is really why we don't have a sense of everlasting happiness or inner contentment. Sometimes we feel that we are happy and in the next moment we feel that we are unhappy. Sometimes we realize that we are awakened and in the next moment we feel that we are not awakened. Sometimes we are as shiny as the beautiful weather and sometimes we are very gloomy just like the weather. Our consciousness is fluctuating between sorrow and happiness, joy and depression, pain and pleasure. Our mind is always oscillating between those two extremes.

There is another state, the state of equanimity. When our mind approaches the state of equanimity then our mind tells us, "This is very boring. Get out of this place." And then we tend to jump into another extreme of emotion or feeling. But right now we are identifying with the conditions, conditions of happiness and suffering, conditions of separation and coming together. When we identity with conditions we are always subject to sorrow and confusion and there is no source of everlasting freedom at all. When you are no longer identified with external conditions, then you are in the realm of equanimity, you are one with your true nature, your Buddha nature that is completely indestructible, perfect and sublime as it is, forever. Buddha nature can never be injured by what is going on right now in your life. It can never be injured by conditions such as illness, getting what you don't want to get, by being rejected or by dieing. Nothing from the outside can injure your Buddha nature. Buddha nature is like a diamond. The fundamental fact of all teachings of non-duality is that there is divine nature in all beings that is like a diamond.

A diamond symbolizes that which is precious, perfect, sublime, beautiful and indestructible—especially indestructible. In the same way your true essence is indestructible. It can never be injured by anything. In every moment you are absolutely perfect because your true nature is indestructible. Your true nature cannot be conditioned by anything. Your true essence is as perfectly sublime as Buddha. So that means that it is the highest thing in this universe. It is the most sacred entity, more sacred than anything else, your true nature that we all share. So if you are able to simply identify yourself with your true nature, your pure consciousness, then all of your suffering is gone. That's liberation. That's it. There is nothing more than that. That's it. Once you identify with your pure consciousness that's enlightenment. That's liberation. That's Moksha. There's nothing more than that.

CHAPTER FOUR

Just Practice:
The Sacred Lineage of Stubbornness

There are two stages on the path of enlightenment. The first is to have a direct glimpse of the truth which is emptiness. This is a very important stage. Meditators have a glimpse of that completely perfect realization of no self and this realization sometimes comes as the fruition of a long time of meditation practice. But sometimes it happens very quickly, under very auspicious circumstances, a fluke, especially when you are lucky. In that sense there is a Dharma lottery and sometimes you can win. Many people have reported that when they were in the presence of great masters such as His Holiness Khenpo Jigmay Phuntsok they experienced a little bit of no self for a short time. In a way that is like winning the Dharma lottery. But realization sometimes happens as the fruition of years of meditation practice.

When you read the biographies of the great masters, you find that they have spent years meditating and practicing. Even Buddha himself spent a great deal of time meditating in order to have perfect realization of the truth, the great emptiness. This is very important. If we have already had that very extraordinary experience then how can we waste our precious human life? It would be a great mistake, a great self-deception if we end up wasting this very precious human life in order to only pursue the mundane worldly perfections after we have glimpsed the truth of no self. Of course from one perspective if we are not engaging in the spiritual path then life is being wasted no matter what else we are doing. In that sense even though you have great accomplishments and have built huge castles, remarkable bridges or other monuments and people remember you years after you die, still your life is kind of a waste if you haven't really engaged in the path to awakening. Whatever you have created in this life, material wealth, power, relationships, none of this will bring about ultimate happiness, ultimate freedom, enlightenment. From this perspective everything else that we do is just another way of wasting time.

And so sometimes we have to look back at our life and ask. "Has life been meaningful or not? Have I spent my life as a meaningful journey or was it again just a futile and meaningless journey?" And we have to meditate and reflect on whether we have had the opportunity of glimpsing that perfect realization of emptiness. Did I have that awakening experience or not? If I haven't had that experience yet then I must do everything, pay whatever price I have to pay to have it. I have to do everything I can even though there isn't any specific list of things to do to make that realization happen right away. Still we have to be ready to do everything and pay any price in order to bring about that perfect realization.

But sometimes we know what we are supposed to do. We have to give up all attachment to the self and when we do that then always the realization happens right there. It is very difficult to get over self-attachment, attachment to ideas and concepts, beautiful illusions as well as dreadful illusions. However when we are really sure and completely certain that the only way that we can experience awakening is through dropping and dissolving attachment then we should be ready. We don't have to have any special prayers. We can always let go of all attachment, even right now, even in this very moment.

Prayer is a very powerful method sometimes. It is very important for us to pray. You can pray to the truth or emptiness or you can pray to the Buddhas and Bodhisattvas even though they are none other than an expression of our true nature. The Buddhas and Bodhisattvas do not reside outside of our consciousness in the ultimate sense. When you pray, ultimately you are not praying to any separate entity. You are praying to emptiness, the truth. Prayer is very powerful. Pray in order to awake, in order to awake right now, in order to awake right now on this spot before you die, or before we continue this realm of confusion further. When we pray from the bottom of our heart with sincerity and devotion sometimes there is a way that all of our concepts and illusions just fall apart, right there, very miraculously, and there isn't any pain or resistance. All of our illusions, all of our concepts, all of our ideas of right and wrong, me and you, separation and connection, past and future, everything starts falling apart beautifully and there isn't any pain. There is no resistance. It is very beautiful to watch that.

Once we have that perfect realization, that spiritual awakening, then the second stage is to integrate the realization into everyday life. This is perhaps a little challenging and difficult sometimes. It is very wonderful to have spiritual realization or awakening as a transformative, life changing experience. But it can be very difficult to integrate that realization into everyday life and this is the place where many people tend to fail. Many people drop off their commitment to spiritual practice completely and then go on back to an ordinary way of life. We sometimes get completely lost and just start being very ordinary. Then we can look at our diary and remember that one time many years ago we had this wonderful awakening experience.

Sometimes we have very high expectations. We tend to think that we should always have spiritual highs whenever we meditate or practice a spiritual discipline. We demand great results or an instant and miraculous awakening of bliss and so forth whenever we meditate. And that happens sometimes when we meditate or pray. It is very amazing. Your heart opens. Your consciousness begins to expand and then you see clearly what emptiness is. It's just right there. It's wonderful. There is no longer any doubt or resistance.

But sometimes meditation practice can be very ordinary. It's like driving an old beat up car that keeps breaking down. It doesn't really go anywhere. This is when we can begin to lose interest and enthusiasm in maintaining our connection with spiritual practice, our connection to the truth. That's the time we begin to lose all of our aspiration and all of our determination. Sometimes we have to be very stubborn. We just have to practice. We have to meditate and it doesn't really matter whether it is benefiting us or not.

Sometimes you see that it is very clear that spiritual practice is benefiting you. I always hear, "Oh, the Dharma saved my life." Many people come to me and say, "Oh, the Dharma saved my life." I have heard this phrase from many people. People are so thankful to the Dharma, so thankful to the truth. People are so inspired. And then sometimes even those people who were so inspired, so thankful once in their lives, end up losing their sense of commitment and losing their joy to continue their spiritual practice because there were periods in which they didn't really find that it was benefiting them at all. It's like taking herbal medicine. It's supposed to help you but so far there isn't any sign.

Four years ago I went to Tibet and I took a few bottles of Pepto-Bismol. The food there is pretty bad especially when you eat in the restaurants. You can easily get a stomachache. Somehow many people got a stomachache after eating junk food at a restaurant. I started giving out Pepto-Bismol and everyone felt better right away. They were so happy I felt like I was giving out some kind of sacred substance. Usually when you go to Tibet people expect that teachers will give them protection cords or sacred pills. They tend to expect that you are going to give them some kind of sacred substance because it helps you right away. So there isn't any difficulty convincing people that Pepto-Bismol works very well but it is harder to convince people that Dharma works very well. It would be much easier to be a salesman for Pepto-Bismol than for the holy Dharma because you have to allow yourself enough time to develop a relationship to the Dharma. Sometimes it takes quite a while to develop a heartfelt relationship. It takes a long time. Sometimes we have to go through this whole process. We fall out of love with the Dharma and then we fall in love with the Dharma again. We go back and forth many times. And after we have gone through this dance, falling in love with Dharma and falling out of love with Dharma, eventually before we know it, we end up developing a relationship with Dharma to the degree that nothing can really take away our faith. Nothing can interfere with our commitment to Dharma practice. And then our life can settle down after that.

People are sometimes so ready to declare that their life is settled down. People say, "Oh my life is settled down." You hear this when people get married or when people get employment or when people graduate from a university. People say, "Oh my life is settled down." Life is not settled down. It is very far from being settled down. But when you really develop this lifetime, unshakable relationship to the spiritual path then you can say, well my life is settled down because from that moment on there is always a sense of certainty and utter confidence in your life even though ultimately there is no certainty.

Everything is unpredictable. Everything is subject to impermanence, death, dieing, and change. But at the same time there is this certainty without really having any certainty.

In the realm of outer conditions there is no certainty but in the inner realm there is utter certainty. And from that moment on nothing matters to you. It's all okay. It doesn't matter whether you are wealthy or poor, happy or sad, healthy or ill. In the ultimate sense there is a sense of okay-ness and this is what we call spiritual confidence. It is very amazing to have this spiritual confidence. It's the ultimate insurance you see. When you have that, everything is going to be just okay in your life. Everything is okay because you have completely realized the truth.

It's good to ask the question now and then, am I okay with everything? Am I okay with whatever happens? When you ask the question you realize that this self, this ego, is not okay with many things, perhaps with most things in life. It's not okay being poor. It's not okay being sick. It's not okay if you think that you are going to lose that beautiful illusion you are holding on to. It's not okay. So this self is not okay with a lot of things. It's not okay not to have absolute control over our own life. It's not okay that life is so unpredictable. It's not okay that perhaps sooner or later you are going to lose this spiritual high. This ego is not okay with lots of things. It's not okay if . . . whatever . . . if people don't show up for your birthday celebration.

Ego is not okay with lots of things ultimately. But when you develop this unshakable connection, this heart connection to the Dharma, and you love the Dharma completely as the highest wealth, the wealth of wealth, then your life is settled down even if you don't have an incredible experience every moment, one so amazing that you just can't contain your bliss and joy. Having that heartfelt connection to the Dharma is the source of spiritual confidence in your life. And ultimately when you are going to confront perhaps the greatest challenges of your life, death and dieing, illness, separation and not getting what you want to get, there is still this okay-ness, this wisdom confidence, this certainty, this non-material certainty.

So how can we develop this relationship to the holy Dharma? Basically we just have to be stubborn and continue cultivating the work of Dharma each and every day. Just keep practicing. That's all we need to do. And we have to be stubborn. Like I said

Dharma is like taking an herbal medicine sometimes the results will not show up right away. Ego wants to have immediate results and gratification. Sometimes the power of Dharma is not visible, it's invisible. Basically this idea of having noble diligence, noble aspiration means having a stubbornness. You have to be very stubborn. You just have to keep practicing. It really doesn't matter whether or not your practice is resulting in miracles or signs of transformation and evolution of your consciousness. You just keep doing the practice out of faith and out of trust. Sometimes you just keep stubbornly doing the practice.

When I was in the monastery in the Golok region of Tibet we had extraordinary teachers, scholars who taught rich and complex Buddhist philosophy and we had Lama Tsur Lo who I would say is one of the most enlightened teachers that I had. He was a master of discipline and stubbornness and he was kind of a Yogi too. He spent most of his life in retreat. He lived at the monastery and he was on retreat. He came out of retreat now and then and gave public teachings. But mainly he didn't really give much formal teaching and he always said pretty much the same thing, "Practice Dharma." That's all he said, "Practice Dharma." Eventually we knew what we were going to hear from him. And he was kind of grouchy too. He was very old and kind of unattractive in an ordinary sense. He was rather wrathful so everybody was afraid of him. He was not abusive but he was wrathful. In the beginning we learned lots of things from him. Later after we had been studying these great, brilliant compositions we realized that actually we knew more about Buddhism than he did, but we kept going to see him whenever we had time. I was wondering why I kept going to see him. He always said pretty much the same thing, "Practice Dharma" and in addition to that he was grouchy. But then I realized that everything he said to me left a great impression on my mind. He helped me maintain my connection to practice just because he kept saying, "Practice Dharma.

Practice Dharma." He didn't have many students. It's no wonder why. It's an easy way to get rid of students. Just keep telling them practice Dharma, practice meditation. Students come to teachers with this sense of aspiration and most of them are in a good mood. Suddenly the teacher tells them practice Dharma, practice meditation without giving any revolutionary answers or mind blowing enlightening teachings and then we don't want to see these people any more. So that's all he said, and that's all I want to say to you. I feel that I am trying to keep the lineage alive, this sacred lineage of stubbornness.

I want to encourage everybody to meditate. That's what I really want to say. Keep practicing not because you have some commitment to a particular teacher or to a tradition. It's not really about that. Sometimes we have this idea that I am practicing because I have this commitment to a particular teacher or a particular lineage or a particular group. Of course that is a good reason but it is not a complete reason. We have to find ways to convince ourselves to practice not because we have a commitment to a teacher but because we have unconditional love for the spiritual path, because we desire liberation more than anything else, because we desire complete awakening more than anything else. That's why we are practicing. That's the right reason.

If we are practicing only because we have a commitment to a teacher or to the community that's kind of tricky because sometimes we run into troubles and difficulties in our relationships with teachers and communities. These relationships fall apart sometimes and then people tend to throw everything away. The Western expression is to "Throw the baby out with the bathwater." People do that quite a lot especially in the West. So we have to find a reason, a true reason for doing spiritual practice. I am practicing because I have true undieing devotion, undieing passion for awakening. That is a very good reason. When that is the only reason you are practicing then there are no circumstances that can jeopardize your practice. Nothing will distract you from your spiritual practice.

Just keep practicing Dharma every day. Whatever your practice is, silent meditation or prayers just keep doing it every day with utter devotion, utter trust and with a sense of discipline. Discipline is very important. Be completely mindful and present whenever you meditate, whenever you pray. You keep doing that and eventually you don't even care whether or not you are getting anything out of your practice. You just enjoy doing the practice every day. It's like drinking a nice tea every day. We just love drinking it. You are enjoying yourself. You find great joy and richness while you are doing practice. And then when you are not seeking it, awakening, transformation, everything keeps coming your way. We have to be very stubborn in maintaining our commitment to the practice. So I want to encourage everybody, strengthen your commitment to practice.

In Tibet there are many serious meditators like the nuns and monks at Khenpo Jigmay Phuntsok's monastery. Many of them have very small places, just one tiny room with a stove, a small bed and a little altar. Many of them are living a life of simplicity and poverty too. But when you visit the houses or the caves of those serious meditators there is so much bliss. Right away you feel the power of their devotion, their discipline and their commitment to Dharma practice. There is so much bliss. I've heard for example that when people walk into His Holiness Khenpo Jigmay Phuntsok's monastery that there is this wave of blessings that comes as a wave of heat and people can feel it the moment they put their feet on the ground. They feel this ocean of blessing. Everybody feels it whether they are meditators or not. Everyone can feel that energy. It's their blessing as well as the manifestation of their awakened mind.

Many teachers have said that it takes six months for most people to have a genuine transformation through spiritual practice.

This means that you have to be stubborn for six months if you can't be stubborn for your whole lifetime. It's hard to be stubborn with Dharma for a whole lifetime. What they are saying is that you have to be stubborn and practice the Dharma for six months and then most probably after that you are going to come close to an amazing transformation. You realize that there is another world, a transcendent world. There is another way to live. There is another source of happiness. It's almost like we have to make this sudden shift in our perception of what the meaning of life is, what happiness is, what freedom is. You realize, "Oh, now I came to this sudden realization that happiness or freedom is no longer dependent on outer circumstances but rather it depends on consciousness, it depends on Dharma, it depends on the work of Dharma." It's amazing. It's almost like you walked into a new world. Even though you are still living on this planet in this body, you feel like you have moved into a completely different world, one that is much nicer, more peaceful.

CHAPTER FIVE

No Self, No Problem:
Ultimate Awakening

There are quite a few ideas about what it takes to realize enlightenment. Some people say it takes a long time to be awakened and some people say it takes a very short time to be awakened. Some people say there are ten miles between you and enlightenment and some people say there are a billion miles between you and enlightenment. Sometimes it is hard to decide which is the correct perspective.

What is liberation? What is awakening? Actually if we are searching for awakening as a moral reward or as an idealized utopian realm then enlightenment is like chasing after a rainbow. You can chase a rainbow but you are never able to catch it. Perhaps one of the main hindrances preventing us from having a direct experience of enlightenment is our preconceived notion of what enlightenment is. So we have to give up every idea we have of what enlightenment is. Sometimes that can be a little bit uncomfortable especially if we have very high hopes about enlightenment. When we are asked to give up every idea we have about enlightenment we can feel that we are losing everything even our beloved illusion, enlightenment. How merciless and cold hearted. But the ultimate truth or emptiness is the destruction of all illusions and that includes the illusion of enlightenment.

When you meditate, when you just simply pay attention to your breath, then you begin to see that there is an I or a self who is searching for enlightenment and liberation from suffering. But if you keep paying attention to the breath and bodily sensations then eventually all of those ideas, concepts and illusions begin to dissipate one after another. It's like watching a mountain that is covered by clouds. In the beginning you don't see the mountain because it is covered by heavy clouds. But if you keep watching then as the clouds dissolve, the mountain begins to emerge and eventually when all of the clouds are gone, the mountain that was always there appears.

In the same way when you pay attention to the breath and the body sensations and to the awareness that arises, then all the illusions, suffering, confusion, sorrow, personal issues, all of this begins to dissipate. We see that all of these experiences are born of delusion. This is the sense of *I. I* am real and *I* am truly existent. Everything is gone except this sense of self. Then when we continue meditating the sense of self also goes away. When we just keep meditating, when we just remain in that present awareness and observe, then the self dissolves too. When the self dissolves there is just pure awareness. When the self completely collapses there is this inexpressible, simple yet profound and ecstatic, compassionate awareness. Nobody is there. *I* am completely non-existent in that place. There is no separation between Samsara, bad circumstances, and Nirvana, good circumstances. And there is nobody pursuing the path or chasing after enlightenment. In that moment we realize the essence of the Buddha's teaching.

I'll tell you a bit of my personal story. When I first went to the monastery I had all of these fantasies. I thought that it was going to be a journey full of visions, revelations, and angels with flowers descending upon me. Then one of the first prayers that we had was called the Heart Sutra. The Heart Sutra can be very dry to those who haven't realized its meaning. It is not like some of those beautiful ecstatic, mystical verses. The line goes, "There's no nose. There's no mouth. There's no tongue. There's no sound, no smell, no taste, no touch." Anyway we kept reciting the Heart Sutra every day until we had completely memorized it. More than memorizing it, we were able to recite it so fast it was unbelievable. Then one day many years after I had been memorizing and reciting the Heart Sutra I finally came close to a sense of affinity with the meaning of the Heart Sutra and the meaning of this notion that there is nothing there in the ultimate sense. There is not even emptiness. Emptiness is gone too. Having even a glimpse of that understanding was very transformative.

The very essence of Dharma is about dissolving our attachment to the self, and about dissolving every attachment to form, sound, smell, taste, touch, good and bad ideas and all concepts. It is about dropping off all attachment without exception. We often say in Buddhism that one has to be a renunciate in order to bring about awakening or complete liberation in one lifetime. When we say renunciate we are not really speaking about becoming monks or nuns officially or externally but more about becoming monks or nuns internally. Just like Saraha. Saraha was one of the most enlightened persons in the Buddhist tradition. Officially he was a monk in the beginning. He served as a spiritual tutor to one of the Indian kings. But one day he had a relationship with a woman and they kicked him out of the Palace. He sang a very beautiful song of realization. He sang,

> Until yesterday I was a fake monk.
> From now on I am a supreme monk.
> I am the greatest monk.

What he is saying is that he is now a monk internally. He is a renunciate internally. Therefore the ultimate way of becoming a renunciate is by giving up attachment internally. Attachment to everything not just attachment to Samsara and the things that we don't like but attachment to Nirvana and the things that we love too, because when you are attached to Nirvana that is just another way of lingering. It's another way of sustaining this flimsy ego. Therefore we have to give up attachment to Nirvana and to every form of ego because ego takes all kinds of forms. Sometimes ego can even take the form of spiritual phenomena. For example if I truly believe that I am one of the best meditators that's another way of sustaining ego.

Khenpo Tsultrim Lodro is residing in Tibet right now. He is the Dharma regent of His Holiness Khenpo Jigmay Phuntsok and he is very loved by everybody in Tibet. He is a very pure, authentic monk internally as well as externally. But he didn't start becoming a Dharma teacher because he was recognized as a reincarnate Lama or because he had a special privilege. When he came to the monastery His Holiness Khenpo Jigmay Phuntsok asked him to collect the human excrement. He was pointed out directly by His Holiness and specifically designated for this job from among a thousand monks and nuns. This was a new monastery built maybe twenty years ago and there was no toilet system. So he was asked to collect the human excrement. He served as the collector of human excrement for years and years. And now he is the Dharma regent and he is one of the most beloved Dharma teachers all over Tibet. His Holiness Khenpo Jigmay Phuntsok later said, "The moment you showed up at my monastery I knew that you were going to be one of the most beloved Dharma teachers but you had lots of inner obscurations. Until they were purified you could never be who you really are. Therefore I gave you that assignment. I didn't give you that assignment because I thought you were the underdog. You were filled with potential and now you are an accomplished master."

So he is now the Dharma regent and he is leading thousands of people on the perfect, unmistaken path of holy Dharma. His main activity is buying lots of animals, yaks, fish and so forth that are going to be slaughtered. He collects donations from many wealthy as well as poor people and he donates all of this money to release animals that are going to be slaughtered. That is his main work right now.

Ultimately we must dissolve pride and and all of the defense mechanisms of ego such as self-attachment. This includes spiritual pride too because sometimes ego just pops up and manifests in different forms, in camouflage. Therefore true liberation requires the complete renunciation and transcendence of ego, the self. Now you may think, "Oh, am I hearing the same assignment again, this whole idea of eradicating attachment to the self? I have heard this so many times. More than that I have failed so many times with this assignment. I actually came here to look for a different kind of assignment. I still want enlightenment but not this assignment." Ego says, "I still want enlightenment very much, more than anything else but without this whole assignment about eradicating self attachment, ego. I will do anything except that. Please let me have a little opportunity to bargain. Come on, don't be so stubborn."

You see ego initiates that kind of dialog, like bargaining, divine bargaining with the truth. Ego wants to do a little divine arguing with the truth. "You can ask me to do anything including jumping off a cliff. Whatever. I will restrain my sexual impulses. I will do anything, just not that one. That's the last one that I can do. I am not able to do that because that means I have to die. I have to completely die into the great unknowable truth." But you see once again we start wiggling around this last assignment the dissolution of self or melting into emptiness. But whatever you call it that's the only way. There isn't any other way. There is no way to actually bargain with the truth, emptiness, and the more you realize the truth the more you realize that there isn't any other way.

The only way that you can bring about perfect, total awakening right now in this moment is by dissolving the self. There is a painful way of dissolving the self and an ecstatic way of dissolving the self. Dissolving the self in an ecstatic way is known as the path of bliss. The reason that we call it the path of bliss is because it involves not a painful but rather a more ecstatic way of dissolving the self. That's a very good idea isn't it? So how do we dissolve the self blissfully not painfully? When we try to wage a holy war as a means to eradicate this empire of ego we won't be very successful in the end.

As spiritual practitioners, especially as Buddhists we have been declaring war with ego and we have been blaming all of our problems and confusions on ego. Ego is like this nasty and hated scapegoat. "It's my ego," we say in common language. "I'm fighting with my ego." Or "My ego is very strong." Or "My ego is tricking me." We blame everything on ego as if it were a separate entity. We have been having this long holy war with ego, trying to eradicate it. Sometimes we feel that we are winning the war and sometimes ego is wining the war. It is exhausting to constantly fight against ego. And sometimes the very self that is fighting ego is actually ego. That's even trickier in many ways. Sometimes when we are in this heavy holy war, trying to smash and bash ego, if you look right there, directly into your consciousness and inquire who is fighting against ego, it turns out to be ego itself, the I. Therefore the path of bliss is not really about declaring war with ego and trying to get rid of it. Rather it is about allowing the self to dissolve. It is about dissolving the self effortlessly and spontaneously.

How do we do that? There are many, many ways to do that. Sometimes we just rest and that is all that we need to do. In

Buddhist teachings meditation is defined as the art of resting. When you rest you pay attention to the breath, you pay attention to the body sensations. In the beginning you begin to see this huge empire of self, of concepts and ideas. But if you keep paying attention to that present awareness, that peace and serenity, then slowly that empire of ego, that big castle of self-illusion, just begins to disappear. In that moment *I* is already gone and what's revealed is pure luminous awareness. It spontaneously appears, just like the mountain appeared when the clouds dissolved. Your true nature is Buddha mind. In that place there is no self, there is no other. And you know that experientially not conceptually. You know that directly and without any doubt. You just know who you are. You just know your true nature right there with complete confidence. It's extraordinary when you glimpse that.

Sometimes when we just sit and pay attention to the breath, ego comes up and tries to jeopardize our path. Ego will tell you, "Well this is too simple. You are doing nothing that is holy or sacred. This is just paying attention to breath. There are no fireworks right now. There is no special factor right now. This is not going to lead you anywhere." Ego is always trying to seduce you to chase after more beautiful exotic illusions. If you just surrender and remain in that present awareness, pay attention to the breath and be content with that simple awareness then amazingly the self dies. Then there is no longer a self who says, "I don't like what is going on. I don't like this ordinary moment. I don't like just sitting here paying attention to breath." The *I* who doesn't like what is unfolding is completely gone and that is all that matters in the ultimate sense.

When self dissolves then from that moment on everything is already awakened. Trees are awakened, rocks are awakened, birds are enlightened, and clouds in the sky are enlightened. When the Buddha had this moment of complete realization he discovered that this whole universe is already enlightened. More than that he realized that every particle on the ground is also enlightened and he saw that every particle is a Buddha paradise. In each particle there are billions and trillions of Buddha paradises. In each of those particles there are billions of Buddhas residing. This whole universe becomes suddenly enlightened and perfect as it is.

That does not mean that we are going to be completely lost in some kind of spiritual trance, losing our sense of common intelligence, driving through red lights, wearing socks on our head and so forth. Of course ego will tell you not to completely surrender your ordinary, self-grasping mind because there will be a retribution. Ego is always trying to warn you not to be completely awake. A little bit is okay but not completely.

I was reading a story recently. This mother started knocking on the door of her son and she shouted loudly. "My son it is time to wake up. Time to get out of bed. Time to go to school." He said, "No, I don't want to wake up." She kept knocking on the door. Finally he said, "Well I'm awake but I don't want to get out of bed." She said, "Well, you have to get out of bed. You have to go to school." He said, "No. I don't want to go to school." Mother said, "There are three good reasons why you have to go to school. The first reason is that it is time to go to school. The second is that there is a whole school full of kids who are relying on you, and the third reason is that you are forty years old and you are the headmaster. These are three reasons why you have to wake up and go to school."

As meditators we can relate to that person. When we have been practicing meditation for a long time there have been many moments when we have experienced extraordinary transformations, awakening inside. Part of us really does not want to completely renounce attachment to suffering. We don't want to completely dissolve into that great truth, emptiness. There is part of us that wants to hold on to that last attachment. We want to awake a little but not completely. It's convenient for ego not to awaken completely but this is the only way to liberation. Sooner or later we have to completely awaken. That means that we have to completely dissolve into that great emptiness, the ultimate truth of nothingness, completely without holding on to anything, not even enlightenment, not even confusions about liberation, enlightenment, or truth. We have to let go of all of them.

If we try to let go of them, if we try to get rid of them it doesn't work. It backfires because who is trying to get rid of them? There is nobody there in the ultimate sense. So this is about melting, this is about dissolving the self and when we know how to dissolve the self then liberation becomes effortless. It is like drinking nectar rather than working hard. In general this is a way of dissolving the self ecstatically without any struggle, without any resistance and devotion plays a very important role.

When we pray what we are doing is invoking the mind of devotion. Devotion is about no longer resisting anything. We are no longer trying to hold the composure of this illusory entity, ego or self. Self is always collapsing and dissolving in each and every moment. It is always dissolving if you leave it as it is because it's unreal at the very beginning. It's already unreal. It's already collapsing. When we try to construct and maintain the illusion of self then we suffer quite a lot. We experience insecurity and madness, because we are trying to uphold that already falling apart existence of self. Self is already falling apart. Suffering is already falling apart. And who is working so hard twenty four hours a day and trying to keep our Samsara together while complaining about it at the same time? Who is that person?

There is a little bit of a dichotomy here in some sense. It's confusing too because we come to the spiritual path with a lot of enthusiasm and determination. We are complaining about

Samsara, our misery, and we are looking for liberation desperately. At the same time we must remember that Samsara is already falling apart. We may wonder how can that be? I have been stuck for many lifetimes. This vicious cycle is not falling apart on its own. The question is actually who is the self. Who is the one who is trying to maintain that Samsara? Samsara is really very high maintenance. It costs lots of headaches and heartaches when you try to maintain it. Who is the self trying to construct Samsara? Who is that person? It doesn't exist.

My teacher used to tell me that the only way that one can be a true Dharma teacher is to give up every idea that one is a Dharma teacher. He is absolutely right. You have to renounce the idea, "I am the Dharma teacher." He used to tell me that when you are able to completely transcend and cut through even that idea then you can be a great Dharma teacher. So what he was basically talking about is dissolving that attachment to the self.

Imagine that you have a very strong belief in your identity or role in ordinary society. Imagine that you are a boss or a CEO. Imagine that you are considered a beautiful woman or that you believe you are a young person. Imagine that you are heavily identified with one of those illusions of who you are. See how much suffering and anxiety you can go through just trying to secure and maintain that identity. Many people want to be bosses, leaders in this conventional world. Many people want to be elected as mayor or president of a country because then that becomes their identity. And many people inflict so much pain and suffering on other people in order to sustain that identity.

Throughout history leaders have sometimes served as amazing archetypes or models demonstrating how destructive and dangerous ego identity can be. Millions of people have lost their lives and suffered greatly because of people fighting over a position. What is a position? It is unreal. It's illusory. Attachment to any identity can be very violent and destructive. This is the very makeup of Samsara. Therefore the essence of Dharma is about dissolving everything here, right now without waiting. And again how do we dissolve that self ecstatically? We are just present, paying attention to the breath and then the self begins to dissolve. Sometimes we pray. When our heart is completely taken over and seized by the force of devotion then self does not have any power to maintain its composure and ego just dies right there on the spot without analyzing without dismantling the self into tiny pieces and analyzing whether it is real or not. There is no time for analytical meditation. There isn't any time to prepare to transcend the self. Self is already gone a long time ago when your heart is completely taken over by devotion. In that sense what we are doing regarding meditation practice is dissolving the self.

When we meditate I encourage all of us to have the attitude that we are meditating to dissolve the self. That's why we meditate. Hold this perspective in your mind and let your dualistic mind dissolve for at least for a half hour, or at least for ten minutes. When you really allow yourself to finally glimpse that beautiful unexpected glimpse of the truth in which the self is dissolved it's like drinking nectar. It's inexpressible. We often say bliss. Bliss is good word but it can be a misunderstood. The bliss that I am speaking about has nothing to do with ordinary bliss like the bliss of having nice food or having sensual pleasures. This is non-conceptual bliss, which is not based on emotions but based on awareness. We often say that realizing the true nature of who we are is like drinking that nectar of ultimate bliss. The more we drink the more we are going to be addicted which is very good.

It is not enough to drink that nectar once or twice. We have to learn how to drink the nectar of great bliss from the dissolution of self many times. It is not enough to simply remember having the experience some time ago. In the beginning we should drink this nectar of bliss at least three times every day. That's the assignment for everybody who is looking for liberation. Then as time goes by we drink many times, hundreds of times every day. Then eventually we drink a thousand times every day. Then eventually we drink in each and every moment, when were sleeping, when we are awake, when we are talking, when we are meditating, when we are playing music, when we are reciting mantras, when we are fighting with people. At all times we must drink that nectar of bliss. This is called complete total awakening and this is our goal. This is our intention. This is our highest aspiration.

I remember a very short quote from a Buddhist teacher: "No self, no problem." It is really short but very effective too. No self, no problem. This is so true. There is always struggle in our lives either consciously or unconsciously. Many people in the world are going through lots of struggle, social injustice, violence, war. And even in the most prosperous countries which are in some ways very fortunate because on the relative level they may be enjoying material comforts. There is lots of food; people have cars, telephones, a TV. But at the same time if you pay attention to the collective mind, people are suffering. Some people don't have enough money or feel that they are not beautiful or intelligent enough or they don't have this and that. They don't have an ideal relationship or they are worried because they are not enlightened. Many people suffer pretty much out of inner madness, anger, hatred and judgment. People always suffer out of judgment even if they are not conscious of it most of the time.

When we go beyond the self then we go beyond everything. We go beyond every form of struggle that we encounter in life. For example when I meditate if I am not really ready to melt the self then I am struggling. My ego is struggling. "Well, I want to be enlightened. I want to have that bliss that he is talking about right now. Time is running out. I want to feel good. I want to have rapture but it's not there and time is running out. I want to transcend self but it is not working very well. That's why I am kind of frustrated. I am struggling."

So this kind of struggle is almost pervading every aspect of life. There are times when we are on the meditation cushion where we are looking very holy, perfectly spiritual and we are feeling blissed out. But sometimes we are so ordinary. We are talking on the phone and shouting loudly being angry at someone. It is quite amazing how many roles we go through in everyday life. When we sit on the meditation cushion we are very holy. But when we are driving our car on the highway in traffic, talking on the phone and somebody cuts in front of us, we become very reactionary. We even start cursing sometimes and we don't look at all like the guy who was sitting peacefully in meditation a few hours ago. The idea is that there is always struggle. There is always struggle in different forms. There is struggle when we are meditating and there is struggle when we are not meditating as long as the self is real, as long as we still believe that the self is there. When the self goes away then we are already in paradise and there is nothing to do. There isn't anything to do and there isn't anything to acquire. So this should be our mantra for the rest of our life, *no self, no problem*. Keep this in mind, *no self, no problem*.

I know that in our deepest heart each of us has strong faith, real longing and undieing aspiration to go beyond the self. But at the same time there is a way that we also might allow ego to buy time. Ego is very afraid of its complete demise so it tries all kinds of methods and strategies to buy time and postpone. If it cannot do anything else at least it can always postpone. So it keeps postponing and postponing complete liberation. Therefore we always have to be mindful about that and pray to remove all hindrances from our path. The hindrances on the path are actually ego's resistance to complete liberation. That is the ultimate hindrance. So we pray to go beyond all the hindrances and obstacles that ego casts on us so that we can be awakened as soon as possible and so that everybody else can be awakened as soon as possible too.

The heart of Buddha's teaching is beautifully illustrated in the simple mantra of transcendent wisdom:

Om Gate Gate Paragate Parasamgate Bodhi Svaha

It sounds very nice especially when we don't really know the meaning. It means go beyond, go beyond, completely go beyond. It means in each and every moment go beyond clinging to the self, beyond clinging to concepts and ideas. When the self is completely transcended then perfection is already there, awareness is already there. When the self is completely transcended then you realize this amazing truth, everything is already primordially enlightened. All living beings and all phenomena are already enlightened in your awakened mind in that moment. Recently a few people told me that they were in love with the Heart Sutra and I said this is the best news that I have heard in a very long time. When you are in love with the Heart Sutra that means that you are ready to be awakened, ready to be enlightened because the very meaning of the Heart Sutra is the nothingness of the self, the nothingness of duality, the nothingness of Samsara. That's what the Heart Sutra is all about.

When Buddha had that complete awakening he said, "How marvelous to see that all living beings are already enlightened." We say there are two kinds of Buddhas, the sleeping Buddhas and the awakened Buddhas. The sleeping Buddhas are Buddhas nevertheless. So it is up to each of us. Do we want to be a sleeping Buddha or an awakened Buddha? It's our choice each and every moment.

CHAPTER SIX

Acceptance:
The Method of Effortlessness

There is a strong desire in each of us to live a life that is free from all conditions, especially unwanted conditions such as illness. I'm speaking about the unwanted aspects of human life such as old age and illness. A few weeks ago someone asked me to speak about old age. When he asked me this I was able to see from the expression on his face that he was encountering fear regarding this problem of so-called old age. As long as we are living in this human incarnation it is impossible to live a life that is completely free from conditions that we don't want to encounter. I'm speaking about old age, illness and having different kinds of problems. Sometimes we are so fearful that we have almost phobias. Phobia is a psychological term that means something we fear or dread, sometimes in an obsessive even irrational way. I call these conditions phobias.

Each of us is constantly fantasizing about having an utterly perfect existence, like being in a paradise, in a heaven that is free from every circumstance we don't want to face.

In human history no one has been successful in actualizing that kind of a life. But at the same time we like to keep maintaining and feeding this childish fantasy that if we fight hard enough against reality then sooner or later we will actually achieve this idealized life, a life free from all unwanted conditions and situations. Some people work very hard fighting against reality.

One time I was invited to a party where there were a few people who where drinking champagne and soaking in a hot tub. While they were in these very nice circumstances they were complaining about their life. Complaining at that same exact moment they were having champagne, soaking in the hot tub and right after they had just finished eating a nice dinner. You see this is contradictory. This is utterly not true. In some sense it's a little bit out of balance. These people had everything. They were drinking champagne and soaking in a hot tub. They had just finished eating a nice dinner. At the same time they were creating an imaginary empire of suffering and conflict. What they were complaining about doesn't exist. It cannot be discovered anywhere in close proximity.

In the same way when we think that we have conflicts and hindrances, most of the time we can never actually find out where these conflicts and hindrances are. That's because they are only found lingering in our consciousness. Our consciousness is like a factory where we create all kinds of imaginary problems. It is a big factory. Many people are afraid of pollution. They are afraid of things like air pollution from automobiles, factories, oil refineries and so forth. But un-awakened consciousness is, I think, much more polluting than any of these. It might be useful to visualize that there is a factory in our consciousness constantly producing the pollution of imaginary problems, imaginary conflicts. That is the full time job of this egoistic mind. It is no wonder most people are suffering.

People are always suffering either consciously or unconsciously, especially because they are under this fallacy that if they put up a fight against reality then they will be able to achieve their fantasies. They will be able to achieve this childish fantasy that they are going to have a life that is free from all unwanted conditions including old age, illness, car accidents, not having enough money, being sick, having aches and so forth. Maybe if you look back forty or fifty years from now, if you live long enough, this whole thing will be a memory and the problems that you are struggling with today will also be a memory. Hopefully we will be quite awake at that time and we will say to each other, "I was so immature then. I used to be very deluded. I used to take things so seriously. I really didn't have to take everything so seriously because everything is already emptiness." One day we will be able to say that.

In Buddhism we often talk about the external hindrances and the internal hindrances, in other words the external obstacles and internal obstacles. The external obstacles are the more physical obstacles that we all face. Things like earthquakes, being tired, a toothache, a flat tire or anything that gets in the way of what we want. Nobody is born under such auspicious or lucky stars that they don't have to face external obstacles. We are constantly facing external obstacles each and every day. The moment we wake up, our nose is clogged. That is an external obstacle. The toilet doesn't flush correctly. That is an external obstacle too. Our fingernail is too long. That is an external obstacle. These are small obstacles.

Every now and then we can have a major life crisis like discovering that we are terminally ill or that we don't have enough money to buy food. That happens too. That is happening here to some extent. It is not as wide spread as in some parts of the world where day after day people don't have any food. Either there is none or they can't afford to buy it. People can't feed their children. They don't know if they are going to have anything at all to eat tonight. They have to go out on the street and beg. That is their only hope of getting something to eat. At least most of us know that we are going to eat tonight. So these external obstacles can be challenging especially when there is a life crisis like the death of a loved one or being sick or not being able to meet our physical needs. It is very difficult to be in that position when you don't have a sense of spiritual realization unless you are somebody like Milarepa or Machik Labdron or even one of my teachers Lama Tsur Lo.

Lama Tsur Lo suffered from a spinal deformity. He was completely bent over at the waist and could not stand up straight. He always used a walking stick. He couldn't walk without it. Even with the walking stick it was a bit difficult for him to walk and he walked completely bent over at the waist. But Lama Tsar Lo was truly content and very, very happy. He had great spiritual realization but he was very humble and wanted people to think of him as very ordinary not as a special or holy person. When you have true realization like the great masters you can transcend everything. You can transcend illness. You can transcend every problem that you can imagine and even those that you cannot imagine. There's not one single crisis or life condition that you cannot transcend when you are completely liberated, transformed, awakened inside through the power of cultivating spiritual discipline. For ordinary people who don't have that internal liberation the external obstacles can be very challenging, so challenging that sometimes it can actually push somebody away from the path to liberation.

There is a tendency in us to think that spiritual practice is going to fix all of our problems and we carry these unexamined, infantile hopes and fantasies. When we become involved with the Dharma we see that the Dharma isn't going to fix all of our problems. When we are new to the Dharma it is easy to carry that fantasy. People who have been practicing Dharma for ten years or whatever already know that Dharma doesn't do anything ultimately. If you are very new to the Dharma it is easy to be very excited.

This in a way is like falling in love with the Dharma for the first time. We can have this sense that the Dharma is going to fix all of our problems and we can believe that the spiritual community is absolutely divine. We feel that everybody doing the Dharma is completely saintly. It turns out that this is not exactly the case. The community is not very holy. If you stay in it for three or four years you will find all kinds of characters. Some people are likable, some mysterious, some mischievous, challenging, a pain in the neck and so forth. Everybody has an assignment. Some people's assignment is to push everybody's buttons. We have to have all of them in order to complete our community.

As time goes by we begin to see that all of our life's problems are not getting easier. There is no magic wand. So it is very easy to lose that initial love that we have with Dharma. Dharma is not about fixing all of our problems. We have to let go of all of these fantasies. The earlier we let go of all of these fantasies the better it is. If we hang on to the fantasies then we often run into disappointment and disappointment can sometimes create a huge obstacle in our path to liberation. It can completely draw us away from the path. So we have to remember this and maintain the perspective that Dharma is not really a remedy or antidote that is going to fix all of our problems. It is not going to remove all of our unwanted conditions such as illness, and old age. We are not going to be loved by everybody after we practice Dharma. Even though you are on the path, the world is going to relate to you in the same way it used to. Nobody says, "Oh, now you are on the path of the Dharma. Now I am going to be much kinder to you. I'm going to send flowers to you. I'm going to create rainbows everywhere you go. I'm going to pave a nice royal road wherever you walk." The world never says that to you because you are on the path of the Dharma. Sometimes the world becomes even more wrathful and even more challenging because you are on the path.

We say, "Be careful what you wish for." You have to be careful what you wish for because sometimes if you really pray enough to bring about liberation, especially if you really pray to bring about liberation right now, then the world can be very wrathful and very challenging to you. Because when the world presents difficulties and obstacles specifically to you it means that you are now fortunately having the opportunity to pass through all of your reactions, all of your habits, all of your thought patterns, all of your karmic behaviors and rise above all illusory conditions and maintain the mind of Bodhicitta.

Therefore if you are really determined to discover awakening at any cost then you must also expect and be prepared for the fact that you may run into challenges and difficulties too. Not necessarily always from external obstacles but from internal obstacles too, experiences of doubt, anger, irrational emotions, depression and so forth. Even Buddha encountered a great challenge before his awakening. He had an illusion that he was being attacked, ambushed by the force of Mara, just before his awakening. Even Buddha had to go through those ultimate hindrances before his complete awakening.

So now the question is how are we supposed to deal with outer conditions or the physical aspects of everyday life. The answer is acceptance. We have to learn how to accept what is. This is the number one goal. This is the number one goal for spiritual seekers. Learn how to accept what is. Sometimes we do accept what is. As the great Tibetan saint Patrul Rinpoche said, "When your belly is full and the sun is shining upon you, you act like a holy person but when negativities befall you then you act very ordinary." This means that it is easy to accept the circumstances of your life when everything is going well, when your belly is full and the sun is shining. When things are going in the opposite direction then it is very hard to accept what is. The precept, the discipline that we have to try to maintain in our heart in all situations is learning how to accept, always. When we are not ready to accept, we are completely under the jurisdiction of ego. Then we don't accept anything. We don't accept the fact that we are on this planet. But what can we do? There is nothing that we can do. Ego is sometimes very spoiled. It's like a child who constantly throws tantrums for no reason.

Ego is the problem. Sometimes your ego doesn't accept that you are in this place. Sometimes your ego doesn't accept who you are. Sometimes your ego doesn't accept the way things are without any real complaint. So what do we do? There is nothing that we can do. You see. Sometimes ego doesn't accept the fact that the sky is blue. But there is nothing that we can do. You see. Sometimes it doesn't accept that we are living on this planet that is permeated constantly by natural disasters, earthquakes, floods, accidents. There is nothing that we can do except accept that and learn how to love everybody.

When you accept the way things are then you are able to love everybody. When you are not able to accept even one thing in this world right now then you cannot love because the lack of acceptance is conflict. Conflict is pain. It is psychological pain. It is a spiritual illness. As long as your heart is tormented by pain you do not have the strength to love everybody. Because of that, it is impossible to bring about inner awakening as long as our hearts are tormented by the pain of not accepting the way things are in our lives.

It would be almost impossible to say that I want to practice loving-kindness toward all living beings but at the same time I'm having lots of problems in my life. That's contradictory, you see? It doesn't work. If your heart is tormented by pain because you are not accepting the way things are in your life then it is impossible for you to open your heart and let go of all of your defensiveness. So therefore we have to constantly practice to accept the way things are. We have to remind ourselves to accept the way things are. This is pretty much what the teachings called Mind Training are all about. Mind Training in Buddhism is about carrying those perspectives and even reciting slogans, phrases like "I shall accept the way things are."

There is a wonderful student who writes a slogan every morning when he wakes up. He tells me, "Today my slogan or my practice is to accept the way things are." Or "Today my practice is to love everybody. Today my slogan is I'm not going to get angry. I'm not going to judge people. I'm going to be thankful for everything." He comes up with these amazing slogans every day out of his aspiration, his utter devotion to spiritual practice. In the same way we should turn our minds to reciting and carrying those teachings, those enlightened perspectives or slogans and to say, "I am going to accept everything." When you accept everything then there isn't any problem. All problems dissolve right there. When you don't accept even one thing then a small problem can become a big problem. Just a tiny problem can completely destroy your entire inner peace when you don't accept it.

Imagine that you look into the mirror and suddenly you realize, whatever . . . there is something wrong with your clothes. There is something wrong with your hairstyle. You have nice hair but then one hair goes astray. It is going *this* way and we want to keep pushing it, wanting it to go *that* way. If we take that seriously it can be enough to destroy our whole day. At first it is no problem. Then we think, "I don't like the fact that my hair is going in that direction." Then our mind has the tendency to blow everything out of proportion. "I really hate the fact that my hair is going in the wrong direction. I don't like it. I hate it." And it keeps growing. This dark thought keeps growing and before you know it your entire consciousness is taken over by that dark, poisonous thought. Then it becomes angry. Then you start yelling at people and they start yelling back at you. And it creates this whole problem out of nothing.

When you accept not just the small problems but also even the big ones, then they become very easy to handle. We become like those great, enlightened masters, the Bodhisattvas who were able to maintain a mind of love and ecstasy when they were facing death and dieing. There are many stories about the enlightened ones who sang songs while they were dieing and who wrote the most incredible poems when they were dieing. They didn't say, "Oh, beat that guy who robbed me." They didn't say, "Ask my neighbor to pay back the money he or she borrowed from me." They didn't say anything like that. Rather all of their last testaments are about loving everybody and maintaining serenity. This is truly inspiring in every respect. Is it possible for us to achieve this? Yes, it is very possible. All that we need to do is train our mind to accept the way things are.

As spiritual seekers we don't have to invite challenges but we have to celebrate challenges when they visit us. I am not saying that we have to go around looking for trouble or challenges. That is not our assignment. But when they arise we must know how to surrender to them and accept them. We have to even be jubilant in crisis and think, "Oh this is such an extraordinary golden opportunity to practice how to accept. If I am able to accept this condition at this moment in my life then I will be able to transcend all of my fear, all of my insecurities. This is an assignment given by the truth." You have to almost prostrate to the challenges when they visit you without invitation. When they are actually knocking at your door then you have to be thankful to them. In that sense, as spiritual seekers, we have to take our whole life as our practice, as path. Life is a path. From the moment we wake up in the morning until the time we go to sleep at night our whole life is filled with opportunities for cultivating acceptance, patience, tolerance, forgiveness, awareness, mindfulness.

You don't have to be in any special place to practice Dharma. You don't have to be in a temple or a place of meditation. Life is filled with many opportunities to practice holy Dharma. A friend of ours died from cancer. He had an expression that he used when he was going through difficulties. He always used to say, "This is AFOG, another f___ing opportunity to grow." That was his slogan. Not a very nice slogan but it worked for him. I would say another holy opportunity to grow. Let's get rid of that "f" and use an "h." Then we can use that. So this is a good motto when dealing with external obstacles.

Then for the internal obstacles, these are the more intimate issues. Imagine those psychological and spiritual issues that keep coming back. These internal issues keep coming back even after we feel we have resolved them. When we feel that there is nothing left then these obstacles that are almost like demons hiding in our consciousness come back. These are the demons of anger, demons of doubt, demons of loneliness, demons of boredom and they always try to reclaim us every time we are on the verge of completely awakening. How do we deal with that? Ultimately we have to carry this perspective. We have to see that all of these demons are unreal.

Your Karma is unreal. Your Karma is also illusion. Buddha taught that everything is emptiness. Problems of life even though they appear unending and recurring are emptiness and therefore Karma is empty too. Karma is unreal. Karma is not a thing, it is not a substance that you can pinpoint, that you can break down, that you can build into a fire. Rather Karma is internal. It is the state of your mind. It is the accumulation of the body of your belief systems, your thoughts, your pains, and your anger. It goes back many lifetimes. Karma can only be purified by realizing the truth, the pure essence of your consciousness. Karma is not a substance like some kind of tumor in your brain or your heart that you can get rid of by performing surgery.

There is a beautiful story about internal obstacles. There once lived a very famous Mahasiddha. She was a Brahman from a high caste and she was very devoted. According to her tradition she was supposed to bathe her body many times a day in order to purify sins and impurities. So she used to go to this river bank every day and stay until the sun set and bathe in this holy water. There was another hidden Yogini who was completely enlightened and who had the vision that this Brahman woman was going to awaken eventually. So one day this hidden Yogini walked by the riverbank and sang a song to this very pure kind of woman who was taking all of these baths. She said, "You can not purify your sins, your Karma, by washing your body with water. If that were so then fishermen would already be awakened because they are in the water day and night." At that moment the Brahman woman stopped because she was very struck by what the Yogini said. And she asked, "What is the true method of purification?" The Yogini said, "The method of effortlessness." She asked, "What is that?" And the Yogini replied,

> Sitting in the ocean of luminous consciousness,
> Observe all of the ripples without doing anything.
> The waves of thought jump up. You simply watch them.
> They never stay longer than a few seconds.
> They always go back into the water.
> Nevertheless now and then they jump out of the water again.
> You watch them. They dance.
> Then they go back into the water again.
> There is already liberation in this non-doing observation.

So in this poem she said that your thoughts are like ripples and your basic consciousness is like the ocean. So Karma is actually nothing more than thought. Whatever arises in your consciousness, bad thoughts, good thoughts, don't try to catch them. Watch them. It's like watching the waves on the surface of the ocean. They arise and they always go back. In the same way you just observe your mind without any effort. Remember this is called the method of effortlessness. You don't try to alter or change the way it is in relationship to mind. Sometimes you experience the arising of positive thoughts. "Oh today is a beautiful day. I'm about to awake." Or you think, "Oh, I'm wonderful, I'm good. I'm really perfect." These are positive thoughts. We think these out of nowhere, without any reason.

Then sometimes you have the thought, "I'm really terrible. I'm the worst of the worst." Today is a terrible day. The whole world is against me." These are just thoughts, negative thoughts. According to the path of effortlessness, we don't attach to any of the positive thoughts and we don't try to remove or transform the negative thoughts.

Observe and watch without being shaped, without being changed just like you watch the waves rising and going back into the water. They all dissolve. Negativity dissolves, suffering dissolves if you can do that. This is also a more subtle form of acceptance. This is called the "Way of Abiding." The story tells us that through the method of effortlessness this devoted woman was completely awakened.

We should all follow in her footsteps by practicing acceptance and learning the method of effortlessness, the method of no force. No dreams. No expectations. Simply observe. By observe I don't mean concentrating on your breath, focusing on an object, or just sitting there. Observing means being in that non-judgmental realm of awareness. If you know how to stay in that place then you realize that actually you are no longer just an ordinary entity. Rather you are already Buddha. You know how to directly experience being Buddha. Without this what we are doing is simply nothing more than just optimistic Buddhist philosophy. That's what I call it. "Yes I'm supposed to be Buddha but I don't feel that way today. Sorry, I'm not feeling like Buddha right now." The truth is we never feel we are like Buddha as long as we are holding onto this egoistic mind. But when we know how to observe then we know that all of these teachings are true. Our heart opens and is filled with loving-kindness. We feel this luminous acceptance each and every moment. We are in the state of just being without doing, without any effort.

This true path is the method of effortlessness. Our assignment is acceptance. Accept everything. Accept whatever arises. Accept and simply observe in a state of non-doing.

CHAPTER SEVEN

Realizing Buddha Nature:
The Heart of Spiritual Practice

The very essence of each living being is Buddha. That means that the very essence of each of us is divine. This is not simply an idea, a nice concept. This is the truth. This is the unchangeable truth. Now and again when our hearts are completely open and we surrender to that inexpressible truth then we realize that we are all Buddhas. All living beings are Buddhas. In that realm of perfect realization it is quite easy to experience loving-kindness, compassion, forgiveness and acceptance, acceptance of who we are as well as acceptance of others. And it is quite liberating to have even a momentary glimpse of one's nature as a Buddha because then we see how illusory our suffering is and how perfect everyone is. It is very easy to have that blissful realization when you know that your true nature is Buddha.

Of course we cannot force ourselves to realize our true nature but we have to create the space each and every day to glimpse this Buddha nature, this universal Buddha nature, this cosmic Buddha nature. Not just our own Buddha nature but also the Buddha nature of all living beings. We must allow ourselves to have this realization once every day or a few times every day otherwise it is like going the whole day without drinking any water. Our consciousness ends up being very thirsty and when it is thirsty then it's grouchy. When it's grouchy then it is kind of violent and so we start accumulating new Karma.

It isn't very productive if you just remember that you had that perfect realization of your true nature once many years ago. "Oh yeah. I know what he is talking about. He's talking about that experience I had six years ago. That was pretty cool. It was delicious to experience. It was liberating, but in the past six years I haven't had any more experiences like that;" or "I had that experience when I visited a very sacred place;" or "I had that experience fifteen years ago when I visited an extraordinary teacher." It is really important to allow yourself to have that perfect realization every day. The quality of our spiritual practice is determined by the extent to which we can live out of this realization each and every day. When we live out of that realization of Buddha nature that means our spiritual practice is going very well regardless of whether anyone gives us affirmation or approval. We always like to get approval about our practice. I, myself, had a very strong desire to get approval about my meditation practice from my teachers and my community. I always shared about my practice with my teachers hoping they would tell me, "Yes, your meditation is going well." Whatever that means. Part of me didn't really care whether my meditation was going well or not. I just had to hear those words. Praise from somebody I held in high regard, an authority. Then my ego started dancing and I felt like I was a good boy, a good son. I didn't really have any idea whether my spiritual practice was going well or not. My ego just wanted approval.

This is not really about merely seeking approval from a higher authority, a teacher or a parent. Meditation is really about realizing each and every moment that there is an amazing, sublime, exalted reality pervading the entire universe, everything, including you and me and all living beings. Buddha nature pervades everything. Buddha nature pervades all beings. The vital point is that we have to live out of that realization. That is the only reason we are practicing a spiritual discipline in the first place.

When we don't know how to manifest that realization of Buddha nature in our life every day then we really miss the whole point. We completely miss the point of being on this path. And it is quite easy to miss the point sometimes because there are so many spiritual trappings out there. Sometimes it is very difficult to hear the truth. We have a very old expression in Tibet, "Dogs don't like sticks and people don't like the truth." I guess people used to beat dogs with a stick and so dogs don't like sticks. In the same way people don't like the truth. It can be very hard to hear the truth, the truth about our spiritual practice and the truth about our illusions. When there are things we don't want to hear and if the teachings get too challenging then we sometimes think that it is a good idea to find another teacher. Then we come up with many reasons why finding a new teacher is a good idea.

When I was growing up in Tibet we didn't have a lot of candy. Now there is plenty of sweet candy in Tibet but that wasn't the case when I was growing up. We lived very simply and had candy only once or twice a year. Many of the children, including me, loved candy but it was hard to get. We had a doctor in our village who gave out cough medicine that was extremely sweet so we were very happy whenever we got a cold. We'd start coughing and pretty soon we'd go to the doctor and get that sweet medicine. We loved it so much that sometimes we pretended that we were sick. One time I pretended that I was sick, that I had a cough. My grandfather took me to the doctor and this time the doctor said, "I'm sorry we don't have any more of that sweet medicine right now but we have another medicine." She gave me this new medicine that was extremely bitter. I told my grandfather that I wasn't going to take it because it was too bitter. But my grandfather said, "You're sick. You have to take this medicine."

Being on the path is like that too. We all want that sweet medicine. We all want to be awakened. We all want to have that amazing, immediate, awakening, overnight. Not just awakening, but blissful awakening. Not just being on the path, but being on the blissful path. Sometimes the truth is bitter. It's very difficult to digest because it constantly demands going beyond our ego. The more we realize the essence of Dharma the more we realize our true spiritual assignment, our major assignment this lifetime, is going beyond our ego. The only way to liberation is going beyond our ego. There isn't any other choice. There isn't another path. That's the only way. Of course there are a few different ways of going beyond ego. You can go beyond ego painfully or you can go beyond ego with great bliss.

For some people the path is quite painful because the whole process of going beyond ego can be quite challenging. It can be exhausting and discouraging. It almost feels like you are wrestling and fighting with ego and sometimes you bruise ego and sometimes ego bruises you. Every time a teacher talks about going beyond ego there is someone who says, "Please no. Not that again. Leave me alone today. I already have enough problems. I don't want to hear this stuff about eradicating ego." Going beyond ego is absolutely about how much you are surrendering to love. If you are surrendering to Buddha nature, to the truth, then it is so easy and so spontaneous to go beyond ego. There's no struggle. When you are really surrendering, when you are really in the heart of surrendering to the truth then it is easy to go beyond everything. Go beyond this life. Go beyond confusion. Go beyond hope and fear. Go beyond fear of old age, fear of sickness, fear of not being wanted. It is so easy and so spontaneous to go beyond everything when you really surrender to the truth.

When you are not ready to surrender to the truth then eradicating ego can be perhaps the most challenging work that you can ever undertake. It can be just hopeless. There's not much hope as long as you want to hold onto this idea of not surrendering to the truth because we want to protect this illusion of self and we want to secure our own version of reality. We all have our own version of reality and we want to protect that. We don't want to let go of that. Surrender means that we just let go of everything without really worrying about the consequences. But ego is always sending these messages that we really do have to worry about the consequences. Ego is basically always trying to convince us not to let go. "If you let go of everything then what will you do with your life? You won't have any certainty. You will be lost. You won't have any security. You won't have any insurance. What will happen to you if you let go of everything?"

Here there is no written guarantee. When you buy something from the store there is a guarantee and if it doesn't work you can take it back for a refund. It's not like that. There is no guarantee. There is no policy that says if eradication of ego doesn't work then you can have ego back. You can have everything back. You can have all of your beautiful reasons back. As long as you are looking for that guarantee then you will never know how to transcend ego, this false sense of self. Letting go of ego, letting go of everything means not being attached to anything. It means going beyond everything as if you were going to die. On this path you just let go of everything. You let go of the bad illusions as well as the beautiful illusions including spiritual growth, enlightenment and transformation. You let go of all of it, right now. You even let go of the self who is trying to talk you into having a second thought about it, or tying to talk you into at least getting a guarantee. You let go of all of it immediately as if you were going to die in this moment, as if you were going to jump off an airplane without a parachute. Then in that moment, miraculously, you are already awake and your true nature is already realized. You are a realized one in that very moment when there is no longer resistance. When there is the readiness to surrender to the truth, then the path of awakening is quite blissful. This is known as the path of Mahasukha, the path of great bliss.

So we have to work with this whole issue of resistance and learn how to surrender. We have to look into our consciousness when we meditate or when we pray and see what is blocking us from surrendering to the truth. Sometimes we can ask teachers or spiritual brothers and sisters to tell us what our resistance is. It is wonderful to pray to the truth and ask what our resistance is. If you have the willingness to acknowledge resistance you will see immediately what it is blocking you from awakening to your true nature. Right away you see. Therefore whenever you want to go beyond resistance but you are not seeing what your resistance is, one of the best things that you can do is to pray. You will always find that the truth will help you acknowledge and discover hidden resistance. You will see it immediately.

Sometimes you will find that your resistance is actually suffering. You have been suffering without knowing it. Sometimes you will see that the resistance is pride, the sense that I'm really a better person than anybody else. I'm a very amazing meditator or I'm a great teacher or I'm wealthy or I have a Ph.D. or my religion is better than other religions or my path is better than other paths. That's a form of pride, isn't it? I'm more talented than other people or I'm beautiful. That's pride. You realize that pride has been the resistance. Then sometimes you realize that your resistance has been hatred. You realize that you have been hating others for a long time, perhaps many lifetimes. Perhaps you have been hating your parents, your enemies, your neighbors or even a whole group of people because of their belief system, their lifestyle or their traditions. You may even realize that you have been hating yourself, feeling that you are inadequate, that there is something wrong with you. I think that many people have this guilt. They think that there is something wrong with them. They don't know what it is, they can't articulate it but there is this very deluded belief that something is wrong with them. That is hatred. Sometimes you realize that hatred has been the resistance that has kept you from realizing the truth.

Sometimes you realize that the resistance has been fear. You have been enslaved by fear without knowing it. You have been afraid of death, old age, afraid of not being wanted by others. Some people are afraid that the end of the world is coming very soon. I recently heard about a man who lived in the mountains. He had a lot of money and was building an underground house stocked with food. He was convinced that there was going to be a nuclear war and the end of the world was near. He thought that he and his friends could hide underground. That's one example of how some people live out of fear.

Once you see that the resistance, regardless of it's form, fear, doubt, insecurity, anger, hatred, lack of compassion, is not the true state of your consciousness at all, then it is very easy to transcend that. These internal issues, emotional defilements, are not who you are. They are like clouds on your consciousness. They are merely temporary conditions on your pure consciousness. They are like stains on your clothes. They are like clouds in the sky. They are like dust on the mirror and they are not the pure nature of your consciousness. They are illusory. They are transient. But when you become attached to them they become crystallized. They become very strong and long lasting conditions that obscure your pure consciousness. When you realize that defilements or emotional upsets are not the pure essence of your consciousness, they are not who you are, then they disappear automatically, naturally right there. It only requires this sudden realization that they are not who you are. They are not the pure essence of your consciousness. In this state, where all defilements are dissolved and transcended, the only thing that you realize is your pure, primordial consciousness and that is Buddha. In that place you no longer identify with your ego with your false self, rather you realize your true nature. Not only do you realize your own true nature, you realize the true nature of all living beings. That true nature, that Buddha essence is not like your ego. Ego is very individual. There is *my* ego and there is *your* ego. There is no such thing as a universal ego. Just like each of us has a different name, we all have different individual egos. Egos are separate from each other. Sometimes when there are a lot of egos together it causes problems. The clash of egos is not always pleasant. That's why people fight and declare war on each other.

But true nature is not like that individual ego. There is no *my* true nature and *your* true nature. There is only *one* true nature. In that place we are all one. We are completely one. This is difficult to grasp when we are not experiencing that oneness of everything and all beings. From the perspective of egoic mind we are separate from each other because my body is separate from your body, my name is separate from your name and my possessions are separate from yours. My ego identity is separate from yours. But when you realize your true nature then you are no longer relating to yourself or to others from the perspective of ego. You are residing in that non-dual, ego-less, pure consciousness. In that place you realize that there is only one cosmic universal Buddha nature. You realize that we are all one. And when you realize the oneness of all beings it is impossible to hate somebody, or have anger or attachment towards somebody. You realize that you are the Buddha and you realize that you are one with suffering, living beings who are also Buddha. You have been one with all of them from time immemorial.

In Buddhism there is a refuge ceremony in which you take refuge in the Three Jewels: the Buddha, the Dharma, and the Sangha. When we take refuge in the Sangha in general it means spiritual fellowship. But we are not only taking refuge in our spiritual community or fellowship. We are also taking refuge in all living beings because all living beings are Buddhas. We take refuge in the Buddha essence of all living beings. We take refuge in the Buddhas and we take refuge in the living beings who are suffering as well. For example you take refuge in the Buddha nature of the teacher who is giving the Dharma teaching and equally you take refuge in the Buddha nature of the person who is begging on the street, the homeless person. You take refuge in the Buddha nature of all living beings because every living being has Buddha nature and we are one with every living being when we realize Buddha nature.

So the path is about letting go of all of that resistance, about letting all of our defense mechanisms dissolve. Right now is the perfect moment to let all of that dissolve. Sometimes we listen to teachings and we think that now is the time to listen and then some time later it will be the time to do the work. It's not like that. This moment, this actual moment right now, is the perfect moment to dissolve all of your resistance. Actually it is the only moment. There is no reason to wait, no reason to postpone this work. Right now is always the perfect moment. If you are not willing to dissolve your resistance then you are not able to be open hearted. So this moment is always the perfect moment, the only moment that you can allow yourself to go beyond all of the defensiveness, all of the resistance that is keeping you from realizing your true nature. This moment is the perfect moment to do that.

It is good to ask the question, "Why am I holding on to this resistance so dearly? Why am I holding on so dearly to doubt, to fear, to suffering when the truth is I can go beyond all of it at any given moment? Why am I drinking poison when I have a choice not to drink it? Why am I imprisoning myself when I am ready to be free? Why am I hitting my head against a rock when I don't have to do that?" We are like somebody who ties themselves up with a rope and says, "Please stop doing this. It is very uncomfortable. It hurts." But there is nobody there. Nobody is doing anything to us except ourselves. Why are we doing that? Why am I doing that? Why am I so obsessively holding on to these things that are the hindrance to awakening, the hindrance to blissful awakening?

So this is the perfect moment to dissolve them and we all know how to dissolve them.

Let's say that I hate somebody. I really want to hate somebody. I really want to hate myself. Ego says, "I have to hate. I haven't finished this one. Maybe in ten years I'm going to finish hating myself or others and then I'm going to completely allow myself to realize the true nature." This kind of going back and forth and trying to bargain with the truth never works out so we have to stop trying to bargain with the truth. To me the greatest sin is to bargain with the truth. Bargaining with the truth is the greatest sin because that is the only force keeping you from realizing your true nature.

Our assignment is letting go of resistance. I believe that everybody knows how to do that. I have complete confidence that everyone knows how to let go of their illusions. It's pretty much up to each of you whether you are going to truly allow yourself to drop off all of your resistance. When you ask the question, "How do we do that?" sometimes that's just another excuse, another form of resistance. So there is no *how*. There is only *must do*. Drop all of your defensiveness and allow yourself to have that blissful realization of your true nature.

I am asking everybody to vow to practice dropping all of your resistance and surrender to that Buddha nature of all living beings. Drop all fear. Drop all sorrow. Drop all worry. It's like dropping a weight that you have been carrying on your shoulders for whatever, ten million years.

CHAPTER EIGHT

Truth's Eternal Mantra: "Hey, It's Your Fantasy"

What is spiritual realization? Realization means the enlightened mind or the wisdom that realizes the way things are, the nature of reality. Only such realization brings about freedom. Realization is not some kind of exalted state of consciousness. It is not a meditative state of mind. Rather it is wisdom that realizes the way things are, the nature of reality, the truth.

Most of the time we living in an unenlightened state of mind and we never see the way things are. We are often confused and lost in darkness, this inner darkness of not finding our true nature. In that sense the more we are able to be in harmony with reality or the way things are, the less suffering and conflict we experience. In order to find true liberation within, we have to remove all of our mental blinders and realize the great truth, the emptiness or the openness of all things, all situations.

Most of the time our mind is in disagreement with reality whether we accept this fact or not. We might all like to believe that we are in alignment with the spiritual path because we are meditators. But you cannot be in agreement with the true spiritual path unless you are also in agreement with the truth, with reality. It just doesn't work. But our ego wants to have the best of both worlds. Ego wants to be in agreement with the spiritual path as an idea but it doesn't want to be in agreement with reality or the truth of emptiness. That's because sometimes this is rather painful to egoic mind. Sometimes we have this idea that we are in agreement with the spiritual path because we are paying the dues. "I am praying every day. I am meditating every day. What else do you want from me?" It's true our ego likes to think that we are spiritual practitioners and lovers of the truth. Our ego likes to think that we have great love, faith and unflinching devotion to the truth.

But we have to accept this very bitter news, this very painful truth and that is that there isn't any other way to be completely, wholly in agreement and in harmony with the true spiritual path unless we are also in agreement with reality. Therefore our assignment is to inquire into our consciousness every day and see whether our body, speech and mind are really in alignment with the truth. That means that my actions, my speech and my thoughts should always be in accordance with the principles of love, kindness, compassion and also the truth.

I am not saying that we always have to be perfect. We are not perfect. We don't have to be infallible. We can't be infallible most of the time, you see. I realize that because my ego always wants to start the meditations at a certain time and end it exactly at a certain time, and it doesn't happen. Sometimes it's one or two minutes early or late so that's kind of showing that we can't really be infallible. We are always fallible. So this is not about being infallible about being some kind of saint or holy person. This is about at least trying to have the strength and commitment to live a life according to the true spiritual path. It is very beautiful when you really start to take this whole assignment seriously, trying to live in accordance with the principles of true spirituality. Dharma is not some kind of cultural cult or some sort of outdated religious code. Dharma is always perfect because it is always in alignment with reality and that makes it completely infallible. You cannot find even one speck of a mistake in the Dharma because Dharma itself is already united with eternal truth.

Therefore it is very liberating not imprisoning when you live according to the true spiritual path. Whereas when you try to live in accordance with a cultural code or outdated religious ethics then it is stifling and binding rather than liberating. But when you live according to the principles of the true spiritual path it is very enriching. It makes you more intelligent, it makes you more open hearted. It makes you a happy and kind person rather than making you more rigid and inflexible and bound to all sorts of unnecessary and ignorant belief systems.

It is always powerful to inquire, to look into our consciousness and see whether we are really living a life that is in harmony with the true spiritual path. It's not just that we are meditating every day or we are sitting every day. Are we truly living in harmony according to the true spiritual path each and every moment or at least most of the day? You may find that so far you have been doing a very good job. If that is so then treat yourself kindly. Buy yourself a nice whatever, a chocolate as a reward. If you realize that so far, in the last few weeks, you have failed with this assignment of living according to this, then it's good to pray to be able to live in accordance with the true spiritual path.

Prayer is very beautiful. I learned from my own spiritual practice that prayer is one of the most powerful forces to bring about transformation of your consciousness. Prayer is so powerful, so heart opening especially when you know how to make true prayer, not just ordinary prayer but true prayer. Prayer in which all of our resistance is transcended.

Sometimes it is very powerful to pray to the truth. "May I overcome this delusion. May I transcend this delusion." When you make such prayers most of the time you almost immediately experience this pure, brilliant awakened mind that is already free from all mental confusion and emotional upset. It's like you are climbing to the top of a huge mountain where you see everywhere very clearly. You see the nature of truth as well as the nature of illusion. Therefore I recommend that all of you pray. Pray to the highest entity, which is the truth. We must learn to pray to the highest truth to liberate us and to see the truth. If you really pray from the bottom of your heart then the realization always happens. The realization that I was speaking about earlier always happens miraculously.

As spiritual seekers sometimes we are a little bit sidetracked by learning all of these techniques, all of these meditative methods. At the same time we also forget to pay attention to this very vital aspect of spiritual practice, which is to be genuine and to be simple and innocent. You have to be innocent in order to know how to pray. If your mind is completely loaded with knowledge, ideas, concepts and pride then you do not know how to pray. You only know how to pray when your mind is completely innocent and pure and not loaded with concepts and ideas. Then you know how to pray.

Sometimes we pray when we don't have any more ideas, any more solutions. When we are at the end of our rope. I remember that when I was crossing the border between Nepal and Tibet, one night we came to a cascading river. It was very dangerous and there was only a little bit of moonlight. It wasn't very bright and we didn't turn on our flashlights because we were afraid of being spotted by others. There was just one log that crossed over the cascading river. I had never walked on a one-log bridge and I was terrified. Even though I wanted to go back home I didn't know how to get there easily. So I prayed at that moment out of fear. And in that moment I forgot all of my meditative techniques, all of my fancy visualizations, and all ways of analyzing mental states. Everything was gone. I was so terrified. And when I prayed I felt this sudden bliss, calmness and courage. I just walked, and I walked perfectly. I don't know how I did it. Of course it has nothing to do with a miracle. It has to do with letting go of all of our delusions, all of our concepts, all of our fears and just trusting in what is. What is, is always perfect. Either you die or you live or you are poor or you are rich or you are loved or hated by others. You are always perfect in what is, in that dimension of actually purified reality.

So therefore I recommend that everyone pray. We pray whenever we are hindered by confusion, fear or loneliness. Sometimes even when we don't experience those gross levels of emotion, we come across stagnation in our spiritual practice. Our meditation is not going anywhere. It's not a major crisis but our spiritual practice is no longer moving forward. Everything becomes mechanical. The prayers, the meditation becomes very mechanical, stagnant. Then it is very powerful to pray until your heart is completely melted and all of your defensiveness falls apart. You discover once again that you are melting and you are completely falling in love with the truth.

I really want to emphasize fantasy versus reality. Lately I have been reflecting on what the makeup of fantasy is. Fantasy is of course a perception. It is a mental formation but it is always versus or opposed to the nature of reality or the truth. Of course we understand the usual fantasy. People say to each other, "Oh that's just a fantasy. That's your fantasy." When you meditate you realize that fantasy is not just a small segment of our unenlightened consciousness. Rather fantasy is huge. Everything is pretty much a fantasy. That's what we realize when we meditate. We realize that everything is a fantasy. The past is a fantasy. The future is a fantasy. Even the present is a fantasy.

Some fantasies are quite easy to detect. For example I am going to live forever. Or I am going to be young forever even though everybody else is getting old. Those kinds of fantasies are quite easy to detect. Maybe I am fantasizing that I am going to receive an amazing reward or that I am going to become the president of the United States. Sometimes we can even catch ourselves fantasizing dreadful things.

When you meditate. When you really completely allow your-self to enter into the dimension of the truth, emptiness or openness, then your mind becomes this. Rather than meditating or observing, your mind becomes one with the state, that means that the meditation and the object of meditation mingle together. In Buddhism that is called non-dual wisdom or non-dual realization. When that happens then you realize that everything is a fantasy. Self is a fantasy. Suffering is a fantasy. Happiness is a fantasy. You realize that this whole universe is a fantasy. Mind created the phenomena and that's all.

When you realize that everything is a fantasy from the perspective of this truth then there is no self, lost in agony or grief because everything is a fantasy. There is no self that is shouting or reacting to this realization that everything is a fantasy. But when we are not in that mind we often experience disappointment and anger when something turns out to be a fantasy. Let's say that I am fantasizing about nice weather and going for a walk. It's going to be very peaceful. I am going to sit in the redwoods or maybe on the beach and I am going to have a wonderful meditation experience. Or maybe I am going to meet all kinds of interesting people. It turns out that the weather is very rainy and I can't go out. If I am living in that egoistic mind then I can experience a tremendous sense of disappointment. Is that very familiar to all of us? That's quite familiar right? We all know that we have been victimized by the demon of fantasy. We remember so much of our life being enslaved by this fantasy.

I am not saying don't fantasize about anything, not at all. It's impossible anyway. It's not about blocking your consciousness. It's not about trying not to think about anything and trying not to fantasize about anything, not at all. That's the wrong kind of meditation. This is not really about suppressing or shutting down your consciousness not to feel, not to think, not to fantasize. It is about realizing the difference between fantasy and reality.

All of us have fantasies. Fantasies can be very beautiful. Our consciousness needs fantasies sometimes and it is okay to have them as long as we don't believe in them. As long as we realize that these fantasies are fantasies. It is hard to distinguish what is fantasy and what is real when we have completely succumbed to this egoistic unenlightened mind. But if we meditate then we begin to realize that the whole thing, everything has turned out to be a fantasy. There is not even one phenomenon, one condition in life that turns out to be a concrete reality. It turns out that each and every condition, all phenomena in this outer world turn out to be fantasy. This is a fantasy too what is happening right now. Right now in my mind I am fantasizing that I'm talking to all of you and I am fantasizing all of you listening to me. And it is very hard for my ego not to believe that it is real. I am telling everybody that it is not real but actually it seems to be real. This voice in the back of my mind is telling me that it is real.

We are afraid that there is going to be tremendous grief or agony if we realize that everything is a fantasy. We are really working hard most of the time trying to prevent anything, any condition from becoming a fantasy. We are fighting so hard in each and every moment trying to have absolute authority over reality in order to prevent all of our imagined conditions from becoming fantasy. We don't like to see it as fantasy because fantasy means unreal, mind projected. I, or my ego perhaps, is truly working very hard to prevent me from realizing that I am also a fantasy. The self is fantasy too you see.

Perhaps the worst thing that you can say to somebody is that it's their fantasy. "Hey, it's your fantasy." It's easy for us to be offended when somebody says that. But that is exactly what the truth is telling us. It's your fantasy. I think truth's mantra is, "It's your fantasy." When you feel like you are suffering, it's your fantasy. When you feel that you are awakening, it is your fantasy. When you feel that something is wrong with your life it's the same, your fantasy. That is what the truth is always shouting and uttering as an eternal mantra, because the truth has only one intention and that is to awaken all of us. So it's divine eternal mantra is, "Hey it's your fantasy." That's all it is saying in each and every moment.

But do not try to get rid of the fantasy. That's a fantasy too. When you try to get rid of fantasy you wind up being very frustrated because it doesn't work ultimately. So this is not really about getting rid of fantasy. When you allow your mind to become one with the truth or in agreement with the truth, in agreement with the nature of reality then you realize without any effort that everything is fantasy. The realization that all phenomena is a fantasy comes to you. You see it so clearly. So therefore all that we need to do is simply meditate. If you keep meditating then you will realize that everything is fantasy.

When we sit in meditation for twenty minutes we notice in the beginning that we have brought a lot of concepts, worry, expectations and simply this sense of self. Then we keep meditating with single pointed concentration. We are simply being in this present moment, even though there is really no present moment in the ultimate sense. We are simply one with our breath, simply one with the pulse of our blood, simply one with the sensations of sitting on a meditation cushion. This oneness becomes very powerful and we realize that everything slowly disappears. We realize so clearly that everything is a fantasy. There is no pain. There is no one there saying I don't want this to be fantasy. I want this to be real. The realization that everything is a fantasy is a very blissful awakening. All hatred and judgment comes from fantasy too. In the realization of this great emptiness, love and compassion blossoms.

I am going to stop talking now but I encourage everybody to meditate for just twenty minutes sometime today. That is all that I am going to ask and I pray that everybody will realize what we talked about today.

CHAPTER NINE

Are We On The Right Track: Compassion And Loving-Kindness

Now and then we wonder whether we are on the right track or not. We ask ourselves that question sometimes. Not every day. We can't afford to ask that question every day because it might spoil our day. Just like sometimes we are driving in our car headed someplace and then we start wondering whether we are going in the right direction or not. It can be a little uncomfortable. But still it's good to ask the question from time to time, "Am I on the right track or not?"

Let me tell you one of my personal stories. Shortly after I received my driver's license I started driving without any purpose, just for the pleasure of driving. One day I was driving with my friend and we got lost. We looked at each other and said, "Maybe we should just keep driving." Then we saw that it was not so pleasant to look at the street signs because they were constantly indicating that we were heading in the wrong direction. It is a little painful to look at the signs when we are going in the wrong direction. The signs are telling us that we are going in the wrong direction but at the same time we don't know how to get back on the right track.

So I am not recommending that people have this doubt constantly but it is very necessary to ask the question now and then, "Am I on the right track or not?" It is easy to think that we are on the right track because outwardly we are following a spiritual path or following a spiritual teacher. That is not a guarantee because this is not enough to be on the right track. We can be spiritual seekers and at the same time we can be very ordinary in terms of perpetuating our own Karmic patterns, anger, hatred, and judgment. Being spiritual seekers does not mean that we now have eternal certainty or assurance that we are on the right track and therefore don't have to inquire into the very nature of our motivation. Why are we on the path in the first place? Where are we heading? What is our motivation? Are we looking for another form of security? Are we seeking another belief system? There is a possibility that we could have an ulterior motive. Perhaps we are looking for a sense of security.

Ego is always looking for security. Security is an illusion ultimately. Ego is like a monkey who jumps off one branch of a tree and then immediately jumps onto the next branch. This ego is always fantasizing about security. Not just security but eternal security. Ego is going around in this universe shopping for eternal security but so far it has not been found. Eternal security is an illusion. There is no security in this world after all. Ego does not realize that emptiness is the only security. Ego does not realize this because ego is this perception that we are beings separate from reality, from the truth. Also ego has this misperception that we have to constantly use effort to be in control of reality so we can be secure because the opposite of security is no security and that basically means death, impermanence and getting things we don't want to get. Enlightenment is not security.

Recently somebody asked me to write a definition of Nirvana from the perspective of Buddhism. At first I thought, "That's a piece of cake. I'm going to write a beautiful definition of Nirvana. Just give me a pen and a piece of paper." But then when I started it took me three days and I still don't know whether I really figured out what Nirvana is. But anyway at the end of my writing the conclusion is that Nirvana is not really security.

Enlightenment is not some kind of eternal security where from that moment on everything is going to be fine and Buddha or God is always going to smile upon us. When you are enlightened you still have to die. You still get sick. You still get annoyed sometimes. You still experience all of life's conditions just as everyone else experiences life's conditions. The difference is that you no longer have strong, ordinary compulsive reactions to these situations in terms of liking and disliking them. Such reactions often produce hatred, attachment, aversion, desire and so forth. So enlightenment is not security.

Sooner or later we have to give up security. This is our assignment. We have to give up any illusion of security. In the Buddhist teachings sometimes we deliberately practice visualizations, meditations in which we invite all kinds of security that ego desires, whatever that means, permanent youth, relationships, anything that you are very attached to. Youth is sometimes very comforting when we are living in this ordinary unenlightened realm. Youth is worshipped so think about youth. It is quite possible to have a very strong compulsive attachment to being young. But youth is an illusion because it doesn't last forever, eventually we all age. Sometimes it is very powerful to visualize that we are getting old. There is a whole set of meditation practices in which meditators visualize themselves being very old, being sick, and dieing. You visualize that your body is being burned in a fire or being chopped into tiny pieces and fed to those hungry vultures in the charnel grounds in Tibet. It is a very powerful visualization in terms of accentuating all unreasonable attachment to youth and being young and also it is a way of cutting through attachment to this sense of security.

Think about security in terms of relationships, relationships between men and women, teachers and students, between groups, countries and so forth. There is really no ultimate security. Think about money, success, and career. Nothing is permanent. Everything is appearing and disappearing. Everything in this existence is the miraculous dance of divine truth. The truth is always dancing. It never takes a break. The truth is dancing day and night, eternally from the very beginning without any end. Everything is manifested in this dance. The dance is not static. It is constantly in motion, appearing and disappearing, coming together and moving away. So if we are not ready to accept the truth that this existence is always in motion, always changeable, always transient, then we have a big problem. We have a problem not just with ourselves. We have a problem with the truth. You know sometimes people say, "I have a problem with my neighbor." That is nothing in comparison to having a problem with the truth. People have a problem with their car or with the president. That's okay. That's permitted. Imagine that we have a problem with reality. Now we really have a big problem.

If we really look into our mind from this perspective then we realize that we do have a problem with the truth. We do not accept that transient quality of existence. We do not accept it at all. Most often we see change as the ultimate state of danger. Ego is constantly trying to escape from accepting and embracing that eternal dance-like transient quality of existence. Our ego doesn't like that dance. Ego loves things that exist and become solid like a rock. Not just a rock but an eternal unchangeable rock. No changes. Everything is secured. Ego hates the divine dance more than anything else.

On the spiritual path first we begin to see where our suffering has originated. Where does suffering come from? Is it from the outside, from physical situations such as birth, death, dieing, old age, and not getting what we want? Or is it generated from within our consciousness? Through meditation, especially sitting meditation, we come to the realization that all of our suffering, major as well as minor, originates within our unenlightened consciousness. It comes from the fact that we are not accepting the nature of existence that is changeable, transient and always in motion. So then if we allow our ego to be the master and dominate our consciousness and our response to the way things are, then we see everything as fundamentally dark. We feel that we have to fight constantly to maintain a sense of security for this I-ness. We feel that we have to fight constantly whether we are sitting, walking, sleeping or waking. We feel that there is always a war happening somewhere in our consciousness. This lack of peace is what Buddha called Dukha or existential anguish. It is always there. Sometimes we are conscious of it but most of the time we are not conscious of it. It does not mean that we are not experiencing that Dukha when we are not conscious of experiencing it. Sometimes we are able to manage being unconscious of this suffering. We do this by distracting our mind through enjoying sensual pleasures, being busy, fantasizing beautiful futures, whatever.

When you really realize that this war is happening then you realize that you don't have to fight so much. You don't have to perform this huge feng shui on the universe. I feel that we are like feng shui masters for the universe. We try to rearrange everything—sun here, moon here, I'm in the center, get rid of the hell. How about that? That's what we are trying to do most of the time. No old age. Everlasting youth. Everlasting pleasure. We are really working hard at that project aren't we? So now we have to realize the truth. Things are changing. Things are not under our control. We have to tell ourselves, "This is the truth." First ego is going to say, "I don't like this truth. I can't allow this truth." Then we give it a few days. Then ego says, "This is too much for me to handle right now. Leave me alone and I will think about it. I may change my mind." So now there is ego and there is also this kind of weak, wimpy awareness arising. And this wimpy awareness tells ego, "This is the truth. Please accept it." And they talk.

Ego says, "Oh no. I'm not going to accept this truth. This cannot be the truth. Truth should be something else. Truth should be according to my definition of what is true. That means there is a possibility that I can control reality. Then I can rearrange the universe the way I want it. More than that there is the possibility of controlling everything so I can even have eternal life, immortality."

The more that we meditate the stronger awareness becomes. That is the beauty of our meditating assignment. Awareness gets stronger and stronger and eventually ego becomes weaker and weaker. Doubt becomes weaker and weaker. Soon you realize that awareness is completely occupying your body, mind, spirit and heart and that you are now completely in alignment with truth. When you accept that truth, that's extraordinary and there is the arising of liberation. There is great bliss because you realize the truth. Not just the truth but the extraordinary enlightened truth.

Then you begin to see that truth is nothing but the ecstatic dance in which you always experience love, compassion, and awareness every time you witness the eternal beautiful enchanting dance. Then you will be intoxicated each and every moment by bliss, the transcendent bliss of witnessing this dance of reality. You realize this existence is the dance of the truth. You realize that everything that is happening in your life is also the dance of emptiness. You are either dieing or you are poor or you are rich. You are either awakened or confused. There is no longer really a preference because you realize that everything is this transient dance of appearances and disappearances. From that moment on you are enlightened when you are enlightened. When you are unenlightened, you are also enlightened. When you are not confused you are enlightened. When you are confused you are also enlightened. There is no longer a strong preference. Rather you are embracing every manifestation, every expression of reality as this ecstatic dance so you no longer have resistance to what arises. Rather you experience whatever arises as a blissful dance. You see that everything is sacred, enlightened, divine. Seeing every change, every manifestation of life as that ecstatic blissful dance. Then we no longer have any resistance or reaction to the manifestation of reality. We are able to embrace everything as a blessing. We are able to maintain love, kindness, compassion, insight in all situations of life whether they are pleasant or unpleasant.

Right now I am simply asking you to inquire, "Am I on the right track or not?" I remember listening to the teachings of His Holiness the Dalai Lama recently. He is so kind. He never really criticizes anybody. He was talking about terrorists but he never called them terrorists. He called them mischievous people. Many great spiritual teachers have said that if your mind is completely engrossed in compassion then you can be one hundred percent confident that you are on the right track. If you are able to hold everyone in your heart, if you are able to love everyone without any discrimination that means that you are on the right track. It doesn't matter whether you have knowledge about Buddhism or not, whether you are intellectually sophisticated or not, whether you are a beginner or not, or whether you have paid all of the dues or not. You know that you are on the right track because your heart is blessed by compassion and loving-kindness.

On the other hand if our heart is becoming bitter, angry, judgmental and arrogant, if we are creating unnecessary separation between ourselves and others, if we are becoming sectarian, thinking that we are better than others, thinking that we are the chosen people, that means that something is not working with our practice. Therefore it is always good to check one's mind. When we realize that our heart is hardened by judgment and separation, then we must pray. Pray to emptiness which is the truth. Pray for your heart to be blessed, to be opened. And your heart will always be opened because you are praying to the truth that is most exhalted. Ultimately you are praying to what is always residing within you. It is always residing in you, day and night, in each and every moment. Your heart is the hidden paradise. Sooner or later you have to find the golden key and open the door to that hidden paradise in you. If you are looking for a paradise outside of your consciousness then you'll be wandering endlessly in this realm of illusion.

So you have to remember eventually there is this hidden enchanted paradise, your heart. That is the land of bliss, this pure consciousness that is very loving and forgiving, that does not know how to judge you or anybody else. It is always ready to bless you. Actually it is already granting a shower of blessings on you. We are hiding under this shell of ego, protecting ourselves from that divine rain. We are afraid of that rain because it is going to destroy all of our illusions. So we are hiding constantly under the shell of ego, trying to escape from the divine shower. We are being blessed in each and every moment so we don't have to do anything ultimately. We don't have to go anywhere. All we have to do is come out of that shell called ego and let ourselves take a breath. Let yourself take a break from this judgmental, angry, hateful ego and then you will experience your true nature, compassion and loving-kindness.

Ultimately life is very short. Even though we may live another one hundred years still that is very short. We don't have time to hate anybody. We don't have time to judge anybody. So how are we going to spend the rest of our life from this moment on? It is good to ask yourself this question. "How am I going to spend the rest of my life from this moment on?" You must realize that life is extremely short. It is like the duration of the snap of your fingers until the time that you die. So you have to realize that there is nothing to gain and nothing to lose ultimately. There are no enemies. There are no friends ultimately. There is not even any *I*. From this moment on the only thing that matters is to live life from compassion, awareness and wisdom. And when you decide that then your heart opens and you experience being in bliss. No matter what is happening outside you are still able to experience bliss because you are able to see that every situation in life is the divine dance of reality. There is no longer an *I* who is constantly fighting against and trying to control the expression of reality and compassion is actually very natural.

I know that it may sound very corny sometimes when I talk about compassion. There is a part of me that says, "Don't say that. It's too corny. Compassion. Yeah we heard that enough. Nothing is new about that. If you talk about compassion you are just trying to be politically correct. Say something that is more esoteric." But compassion is the heart of all of the teachings and so I encourage everybody from this moment on to practice compassion as the heart of your spiritual path. When you are able to go beyond all temporary internal conditions such as ego, judgment and doubt, you are finally able to be in touch with the very original primordial nature of your heart or your consciousness, and that is love and compassion. Love is the ability to see everything and every being as perfect just as they are, like Buddhas and Bodhisattvas. That's love. Love is devotion. Love is when you see that everybody is a Buddha. You are able to embrace and ultimately love everything because love is devotion and acceptance.

There is a little bit of a difference between love and compassion. Compassion is an expression of love. Compassion is like having sympathy for the suffering of all living beings. Sometimes when we see the suffering of others we experience compassion. If we are able to see everybody as Buddha as well as see every situation as the blissful expression and dance of reality then we are able to love everything. From that moment on we are able to also effortlessly experience compassion toward all beings who are suffering, who are in a state of turmoil. But it would be very difficult to have compassion toward others unless you recognize their true nature as divine. When we are able to let go of our identification with the small self, then automatically we experience that we are love, that we are compassion. Just like when the sun rises above the clouds it shines very brilliantly and illuminates all darkness.

One time these two people had an assignment to assassinate a politician. They went to his home and were waiting for him to show up. Every evening he came home at seven o'clock, but on that day he didn't show up at seven o'clock. At eight o'clock he didn't show up. At nine, ten, eleven he didn't show up. Finally at midnight he still didn't show up. Then they both looked at each other and one person said to the other, "I hope he's okay." So this person experienced Buddha nature right there and forgot that he was the assassin. He forgot that the politician was supposed to be the enemy. He lost all of his concepts so he was in touch with reality. The only thing he experienced was caring and loving-kindness. That is the power of Buddha nature, the experience of your innate love.

So I encourage everybody to practice loving-kindness toward everyone from this moment on. I encourage everybody to love everyone and have compassion toward all beings and see everybody as a Buddha. I encourage everybody to love all of the circumstances of life, even illness, old age, and being rejected as this beautiful ecstatic dance that is impossible to bore you.

CHAPTER TEN

Shortcut to Enlightenment: Transcending Thoughts

First we have to come to believe that enlightenment is possible. Each of us can glimpse enlightenment at any given moment, when we are ready. I have said this so many times. As a matter of fact this is the only thing I am ever saying. Sometimes we relate to this idea that enlightenment is possible at any given moment. But when we are completely wrapped up in the powerful forces of our emotions, concepts and habitual patterns we are not really in agreement with this idea. I want to remind everybody that enlightenment is more than possible. Enlightenment is always knocking on your door. And this is not just some kind of optimistic Buddhist good news.

So why are we not awakened in this very moment? What force holds us back from awakening to the ultimate truth? It often seems that there are huge obstacles. But when we look into our consciousness and simply ask what is holding us back, we don't really find anything. We don't find a devil with two horns holding us back from awakening. I always say that it would be good news if we found a devil. Then we could all get together and wrestle it. That would be easy. But there really is no devil. There is nothing outside of our consciousness holding us back from being awake right now. There are no real blocks, no hindrances.

Let me tell you this Buddhist story. One time a husband told his wife that she could not have any relationships after he died. "If you do I am going to manifest as a powerful demon and make your life hell." So when the domineering husband died the wife took his words seriously for months and years. Then finally she kind of forgot and started having relationships with other people. Every time she came home from a date this demon popped up on the ceiling. He looked very fierce and flames were coming out of his mouth. He yelled, "You went out. You had a date." The demon knew the exact clothes the person was wearing, their exact height and so forth. She was terrified and consulted a Buddhist master who told her to carry a handful of rice and ask the demon just one question. Ask him to tell you how many grains of rice are in your hand. So the next time this demon popped up she grabbed a handful of rice and yelled, "If you are so omniscient tell me right now how many grains of rice are in my hand?" Instantly the demon disappeared and never came back. Actually the demon was her own creation. It was not outside her own mind. The story demonstrates that everything is the elaboration of our own mind.

When you start inquiring into what is holding you back from realizing the truth you come to the realization that there is really nothing there. There are no obstacles. Nothing is holding you back from awakening. That is very amazing to see sometimes and this is a short cut to enlightenment. There are many beautiful names of the truth, emptiness, Buddha mind, Buddha nature, and blissful awareness. There is no difference. They are all the same. Sometimes you will be in the mood to realize emptiness, other times you will be in the mood to realize Buddha nature. Most of the time you will be in the mood to realize blissful awareness. We all are in the mood to realize blissful awareness. We all want to have a cup of that blissful awareness until we realize that actually blissful awareness is the emptiness that we are so afraid of.

You may wonder how you are going to awaken? What I am suggesting is to meditate and now and then to inquire into the question, "What is holding me back from realizing my true nature, my Buddha nature?" This is a very powerful inquiry. I am sharing this based on my own meditation practice. This is one of my favorite meditations because it always takes me to the place where I cannot blame anybody or anything for my lack of awakening. When you open your heart and let go of all kinds of theories and speculations, when you are not distracted even by spiritual fantasies, when you simply wholeheartedly and courageously inquire into what is holding you back that is all that you need to do.

Sometimes it is good to just take off your clothes while you are by yourself and shout loudly to the sky, "Who is holding me back from awakening right now? Or you can just ask the truth, "What is holding me back from awakening right now?" Either way you can't find any answer because there is nobody there. There is nothing holding you back and that's why you never really find any answers. If anybody tells you they have the answer they are obviously lying to you because there isn't any answer. Next you might ask, "If there are no obstacles holding me back then why am I not awakened right now?" And when we look we realize that we are attached to our thoughts. That is all that is happening. Samsara is nothing more than just our identification with thoughts. That's all there is. There is nothing there except thoughts you see.

I met with this veteran of the Vietnam War many years ago in a small town in Louisiana. He was very moved by the Buddhist teachings. He was crying and he said that when he was in the war and he had taken the lives of other people. He felt guilty. He felt that he was a sinner without any possibility of redemption. And he asked me what he should do. Did I have anything to say? I couldn't come up with any words right there. I couldn't say well you did a very good job. So I sat there for a while and meditated and prayed and then finally the only words that came out of my mouth from that prayer were, "Actually that

is in the past. You must live in the present. This is not about con-
doning your deeds. I am not saying that your activity was great
or noble. Of course taking the life of other people is very heavy
Karma in some sense. But in the ultimate sense there is only your
own identification with thoughts and ideas, guilt, and shame.
Let go of it. You have the capacity to be free right now in this
very moment." And so I think that this person got my message
for the time being and he had a smile on his face. After that I
never met with him again. I always hoped that he took that
message to heart.

Look into your consciousness and you will recognize that
your heart has been tormented pretty much throughout this
entire lifetime. Your heart has been always tormented. It has never
been completely at peace believe it or not. That is very much the
foundation of our relationship to each other. We come together
because our hearts have been tormented and we are looking for
a sense of liberation, an answer to how we can transcend the
internal pain and confusion that is always there. That is why we
attend spiritual teachings, why we attend workshops, why we go
to retreats and why we try all kinds of methods and all kinds
of special practices including the strange ones. We do it in order
to find a sense of liberation and freedom from that inner torment.
Our heart has never been completely at peace, completely enlightened, completely serene. I am not exaggerating. If you look into
your heart right now you will see that there is this old ancient
baggage of pain, sorrow and confusion; but at the same time there
is really nothing there except thoughts.

Imagine that your heart is tormented by hatred. Imagine that
you hate somebody because you believe that they hurt you
when you were a child. That seems very much a universal problem in the Western world. Many people have a tremendous
sense of anger and hatred toward their parents. This was a very
shocking discovery for me when I came to the United States.

Many people experience a sense of rage and very strong anger toward their parents and other people who hurt them. Ultimately that is also a thought. It doesn't exist anymore in this very pure present moment. It doesn't really exist. So what we are really carrying is just a bunch of thoughts. When we let go of those thoughts everything is illuminated. So that's all we need to do.

Think about being poor. Think that you are very poor. Start believing that you are very poor. I can really torture my consciousness with these thoughts. "I don't have a nice car. My neighbor's house is much nicer than my house. I don't have the things that I need." Then I can try to get more money and have a better this and that. I can use all of my energy trying to acquire more money, more lucrative work and so forth. Still I will find that my heart is tormented even after I have gained an abundance of material things. That proves that no matter how hard we try to modify the outer circumstances of our life, it never resolves our problems. If I am able to transcend and let go of this sense that I am poor then that's it. My heart is illuminated right there.

Therefore whenever you suffer, whenever you struggle or feel yucky or are having a bad hair day, don't go outside trying to find out what is wrong with your life. Don't treat your life like you treat your car. When something is wrong with the car you have to get out, open the hood, see what's wrong with the engine and fix it. But life is not like a car. Life is consciousness. Life is not something outside of yourself. Therefore whenever you feel that you are suffering, tormented, or challenged always look into your consciousness. Right there, immediately, all you discover is that you are having a very evil affair with an evil thought. That's all there is. Just that thought. And a thought always comes with a specific idea and with some kind of voice, "I am good. I am bad. I am poor. I don't have this. I am not enlightened." It is always associated with a concept and a belief system. Therefore until we are awakened to the ultimate truth we are completely ruled by thoughts. They are always dictating reality to us. So in that sense thought is the ultimate empire of propaganda. Thought is always coloring and defining reality.

I went back to Tibet about ten years ago. People there have very few possessions or material wealth. They have almost nothing. Yet inside many of them are completely wealthy. I brought all of these presents from the United States and then I was hesitant to give them out because many of the people are so pure and so happy. I felt that maybe I was going to pollute their minds. I didn't want to trap their minds because some of the people are so open hearted, loving and completely rich. I have met with some very wealthy people the last few years in the United States and when I looked into their faces they were very unhappy. Yet when I looked at some of those very sincere and good-hearted people living in the countryside in Tibet who have absolute devotion to the path of loving-kindness and wisdom, their hearts are very rich, completely rich. Strangely enough somebody over there who has almost nothing is one hundred times happier than someone over here that has millions of dollars. So that really shows that ultimately nothing is wrong with life.

Both happiness and suffering is a product of our own mind. Enlightenment is also a product of our mind, and Dharma is a product of our mind too. Especially Dharma is a product of our mind. There is no Dharma that will help you until you are absolutely seriously determined to transcend your thoughts. That is what I realized in my own spiritual journey. There is no Dharma until I am really ready wholeheartedly to transcend my thoughts. I can run around, collect teachings, meet with all kinds of teachers named His Holiness this and that, but that is not Dharma. There is no Dharma until I am truly ready to transcend my thoughts. Of course our ego says that we are doing spiritual practice because we are collecting teachings and meditating but there is no real Dharma until we are truly ready to transcend all thoughts, all of the concepts ruling our consciousness. True Dharma is actually the art of transcending your thoughts in each and every moment. True Dharma is not being attached to any thought. True Dharma is cutting through the attachment to whatever thought arises because ultimately everything is thought. There is nothing other than thought.

When you suffer it means that you are attached to a thought. When you feel happy that means that you are experiencing another thought. The very sense of *I* is a thought, too. The *I* that I believe to be so real and concrete doesn't exist, in the ultimate sense. It is just a thought. It is a thought that I have been defending my entire lifetime; a thought that I am willing to defend with the rest of my life. Quite deluded isn't it? I am just a thought yet I am constantly worrying about this *I*'s wellbeing. Is it getting enough sleep? Is it getting enough food? Does it have health insurance? How are its teeth? Has it had a check up with the dentist? Does it have a nice hairstyle? The most liberating, most blissful awareness that you can experience is that you are a lie. Now and then we realize that and it is so liberating. Of course it doesn't happen too many times. Perhaps you have had such a liberating experience. Sometimes those realizations happen when you are in the presence of somebody who is living in that awareness or when you do a lot of intensive practice.

We have always been Buddha. We have been always been perfect. Therefore practicing meditation means working towards transcending thoughts each and every moment. Sometimes it is good to even recite lines, special slogans to remind yourself that Dharma is about transcending thoughts. People often talk about transcending life and death. That is a lofty ideal isn't it? People also talk about transcending Samsara and that is lofty too because how can you transcend Samsara when there is no Samsara? So just forget about trying to transcend Samsara and life and death. Please forget all these fantastic glorious heroic notions.

When we do this we are deliberately making Dharma more difficult than it is because there is no Samsara, no life and death to transcend in the first place. The only thing that you must transcend is your thoughts. Beyond your own thought there is no suffering. There is only thought. This is not simply theory.

What does it mean to transcend your thoughts? It simply means not to believe in your thoughts. When you don't believe in your thoughts you are always awakened. When you believe in thoughts you are un-awakened. That's a statement everybody should memorize. Whenever you are suffering tell yourself, "I am stuck with my thoughts." Then you might like to pray and ask for help. Ask for the power to transcend your thoughts. Ultimately transcending thoughts means not to believe in the thoughts.

This is a perfect moment for everybody to surrender their thoughts, to give up all thoughts, surrender them to the truth. You can offer all of your thoughts whenever you have the mindfulness and awareness. In temples we have a shrine room and the altars are arranged with offering bowls filled with water, flowers, rice and so forth as symbols of the ultimate offering. The ultimate offering is thought. Offering all thoughts to emptiness without any attachment, that is the highest offering. Every time you offer thought to that realm of truth you always experience that blissful awakening.

This is called Ekayana, literally, one technique. This is the highest technique for transcending thoughts. There is really nothing higher than this. This is the very idea, the teaching that I will be speaking about for the rest of my life. So I won't have any further news. No further revelations. This is what you are going to get out of me and my teachings for as long as I am here, the idea of simply transcending your thoughts. That is what Buddha taught really. All he talked about in the ultimate sense is transcending thought. When a Buddhist master was facing his ultimate demise, his physical death, one of his disciples asked him how to present the truth in the simplest language? He said, "Ah. I express all of the sublime teachings in one letter which is Ah." Ah means emptiness and emptiness means transcending your thoughts. Emptiness of thoughts is the path to liberation. It is very good sometimes to review the very nature of your spiritual practice. If your spiritual practice is about transcending thoughts that means that you are on the right track so you should be very happy and you should celebrate that you are on the right track.

But you may discover that your spiritual practice is about gathering more information, more knowledge, more security, especially a sense of security. I think that we all have a desire for security. This seems to be one of the obsessions in the human mind. Sometimes we gain security by developing a relationship with a specific tradition, teacher, or community. In that sense the Dharma is no longer the path to direct awakening. So it is good to renew the very nature of your practice and see whether it is about transcending your thoughts or not. Dharma is about not believing in your mind, about not believing in your thoughts. This is such simple language. Anybody can understand this teaching. Everybody can understand this teaching. Of course we can say this simple message in a very fancy poetic language but the very heart of Dharma is about not believing in this un-awakened deluded mind. When we no longer believe in this mind we experience that ultimate freedom within. We are always free since there is no suffering, there is no death, there is no illness, there is no old age to be transcended in the first place.

I encourage everybody to spend one hour or one half hour where you open your heart. Invite your thoughts of insecurity, hope, fear and so forth. Watch them and then you realize that ultimately there is nothing there except the thoughts of your own mind. And when you let go of your thoughts then you are always free. You realize that your heart is always blissful. Please try to do that.

Glossary

Bodhicitta – The thought or mind of enlightenment, the desire or intention to achieve Buddhahood for the sake of all beings.

Bodhisattvas – Bodhisattvas are those who have dedicated their lives to the path of achieving complete liberation for the sake of relieving the suffering of all beings and helping them to achieve realization.

Brahman – One of the four castes in Indian society. Members of this class are by tradition priests and scholars.

Buddha nature – The essence of Buddhahood in each living being, their true and essential nature.

Dharma – This term has a number of meanings. Most commonly it is used to mean the path to liberation including spiritual teachings and practices.

Dukha – Pain, suffering, sorrow, grief, unhappiness, that which is unsatisfactory. A lack of peace, existential anguish.

Egolessness – Absence of an independent, fixed or permanent state of being.

Emotional Defilements (Obscuring Emotions, Negative Emotions) – The eighty-four thousand kinds of confusion that obscures the mind and prevents realization.

Emptiness – Free from any fixed, independent, permanent existence. Ultimately it is the recognition that Buddha nature resides in every living being.

Golok – The Golok Tibetan Autonomous Prefecture, a region in Eastern Tibet that occupy the valleys and gorges around the upper section of the Yellow River and the mountainous areas of the Amnye Machen Range.

Heart Sutra – The essence of the Buddhist teaching on prajnaparamita, transcendent wisdom. It is recited daily in communities all over the world.

His Holiness Khenpo Jigmay Phunstok (1932–2004) – A brilliant and enlightened teacher who remained in Tibet during the Chinese invasion. He was largely responsible for a spiritual revitalization of Buddhism in Tibet. He started a small hermitage that grew into Serthar Buddhist Institute, a non-sectarian monastic university. Thousands and thousands of teachers have graduated from Serthar Institute and gone on to teach the next generation at monasteries throughout Tibet, China, India and the West.

Karma – The principle of cause and effect. It is also used to mean the result produced by past action.

Khenpo (Tibetan) – The title given to someone who has attained a high degree of knowledge and is in charge of teaching, abbot.

Klesha – See emotional defilements.

Lama – The Tibetan word for teacher, spiritual advisor. Guru in Sanskrit.

Machik Labdron (1055–1153) – The most famous Tibetan Yogini who initiated the practice of meditation called Chod or "cutting through" attachment.

Mahasiddha – A great accomplished Yogi who has reached supreme accomplishment.

Mahasukha – Supreme happiness, great bliss.

Mala – A string of beads used like a rosary.

Mantra – A sacred word or phrase of spiritual significance and power.

Mara – The "demon" that causes obstacles to spiritual practice and enlightenment.

Milarepa, Jetsun (1040–1123) – Tibet's great Yogi and poet whose biography and poems are among the best-loved works in Tibetan Buddhism. He is the archetype of the perfect disciple, practitioner and teacher.

Mipham Rinpoche (1846–1912) – An eminent master of the Nyingma Tradition. One of the greatest scholars of his time whose collected works fill more than thirty volumnes. He studied with masters from all traditions of Tibetan Buddhism and was instrumental in the Rimé or non-sectarian movement.

Moksha – Liberation, spiritual freedom, release, the final goal of human life. Defined here as the recognition of one's identity with ultimate reality and a return to one's original state of perfection.

Nirvana – The state beyond suffering.

Nyingma Tradition – The ancient or older tradition, which presents teachings propagated in Tibet by Padmasambhava in the eighth century.

Patrul Rinpoche (1808-1887) – A prolific author and commentator from Eastern Tibet. Author of *Words of My Perfect Teacher*.

Samsara – The cyclic existence of birth and death.

Saraha – A great Indian Buddhist Mahasiddha of the late eighth century. His most famous work is a trilogy of songs of enlightenment.

Skandas – A Sanskrit word literally meaning "heaps" or "aggregates." The five aggregates are form, sensation, conception, volition and consciousness.

Sutra – A concise text containing the discourses of Shakymuni Buddha or those inspired by him. Sutras are often in the format of a discourse between the Buddha and one of his followers.

Three Jewels – Triratna in Sanskrit. The Buddha (who gave the teachings) the Dharma (his collection of teachings) the Sangha (the community that practices and realizes the teachings).

Yogi and Yogini – Male and female practitioners of yoga or meditation, spiritual practitioners.

DHARMATA  FOUNDATION

Dharmata Foundation carries a complete inventory of Anam Thubten's books and recorded teachings on CD and DVD. For more information, visit our website:

www.dharmatafoundation.org

Or mail: Dharmata Foundation
                  235 Washington Avenue
                  Point Richmond, CA 94801

Anam Thubten travels nationally and internationally to lecture and teach. To join our e-mail list or obtain a schedule of Dharmata events you can reach us at info@dharmata.org or at 510-233-7071.

DHARMATA PRESS

Dharmata Press is a subsidiary of Dharmata Foundation and can be reached at the addresses listed above.